KU-165-879

PUFFIN BOOKS

UNLOCKING THE UNIVERSE

LIBRARIES NI
WITHDRAWN FROM STOCK

STEPHEN HAWKING was a brilliant theoretical physicist, generally considered to have been one of the world's greatest thinkers. He was Lucasian Professor of Mathematics at the University of Cambridge and was the author of *A Brief History of Time*, which was an international bestseller. His other books for the general reader include *A Briefer History of Time*, the essay collection *Black Holes and Baby Universe*, *The Universe in a Nutshell*, and *Brief Answers to the Big Questions*. He died on 14 March 2018.

LUCY HAWKING uses storytelling to help audiences understand and engage with science. She is the co-creator of the George series with her father, Stephen Hawking, which was a global hit, translated into over forty languages. Among the awards Lucy has received for her work is an honorary doctorate of sciences by Queen Mary University of London. Over the past four years, Lucy created two hugely successful projects with the European Space Agency and Curved House to increase STEM engagement in primary schools through arts-based learning. Lucy has made radio documentaries for the BBC and a virtual-reality film with the Guardian Media Group about autism in teenage girls. She is chair of the Stephen Hawking Foundation.

UNLOCKING THE UNIVERSE

STEPHEN & LUCY HAWKING

Illustrated by Jan Bielecki

PUFFIN

PUFFIN BOOKS

UK | USA | Canada | Ireland | Australia | India | New Zealand | South Africa

Puffin Books is part of the Penguin Random House group of companies whose addresses can be found at global.penguinrandomhouse.com.

www.penguin.co.uk   www.puffin.co.uk   www.ladybird.co.uk

Penguin
Random House
UK

First published 2020

001

Copyright © Lucy Hawking, 2020

The acknowledgements on page 419 constitute
an extension of this copyright page

The moral right of the authors and illustrator has been asserted

Text design, illustrations and diagrams by Jan Bielecki

Printed and bound in Great Britain by Clays Ltd, Elcograf S.p.A.

A CIP catalogue record for this book is available from the British Library

HARDBACK
ISBN: 978–0–241–41532–0

INTERNATIONAL PAPERBACK
ISBN: 978–0–241–41886–4

All correspondence to:
Puffin Books
Penguin Random House Children's
80 Strand, London WC2R ORL

MIX
Paper from
responsible sources
FSC® C018179

Penguin Random House is committed to a
sustainable future for our business, our readers
and our planet. This book is made from Forest
Stewardship Council® certified paper.

'Remember to look up at the stars
and not down at your feet'

Stephen Hawking

Contents

Part Four: Dark Matters

Part Five: Life in Space

Introduction

Throughout my life, I had the extraordinary privilege of spending time with, talking to, and asking questions of some of the world's greatest and most innovative scientists who were the friends and colleagues of my father, Stephen. My father was an amazing scientist who realized how important it was to talk about the work he did in ways that people could understand. He thought that everyone had the right to know what scientists did and what it meant. So, to me, it seemed entirely normal to be a schoolgirl who asked questions – and got answers. Sometimes the answers were baffling or thought-provoking or even made me angry. But I got answers from people who knew what they were talking about. And listening to them or asking yet more questions made me feel as though I could reach out and touch the magnificence of the Universe.

When I grew up, I realized how unusual it was to have had this opportunity. If I've tried to do one thing with my work, it is to share the great piece of luck I had in life to have access to these fascinating, original, creative, brilliant and hilarious people by putting them into the books. Starting with my father's amazing essay in our first book together, *George's Secret Key to the Universe*, the whole George series is enriched and illuminated by the voices of these diverse and fabulous scientists and experts, writing about their research and their lives' work for young readers.

Of course, thanks to the internet, we now have lots of information that is more available and much easier to access than when I was a child. But what does it all mean? And how do you know that what you read on the internet is true? My father and I realized, as we wrote together, that we could turn information into knowledge with the help of our 'family' of experts and scientists.

Unlocking the Universe brings all the wonderful essays and facts we had collected together into one book – and includes some amazing new content as well, on topics I've always wanted to explore, such as genetics, the multiverse and a new essay on black holes. Our newest writers also tackle the ethics of AI and the problem of science denial – and our youngest ever contributor takes on climate change and how it feels to be a teenager in a global-warming world.

It seems such a long time since my father and I first had the idea to write about what would happen to a boy if he fell into a black hole. That first book we wrote together was inspired by a question put to my father at a birthday party. That question sent us on a mission to write a book to answer it – and now, here at our seventh and final book, I think we can honestly say that if you ask a question, you never know what might happen as a result. In *George's Secret Key to the Universe*, scientist and Annie's dad Eric is writing a book for kids called 'A User's Guide to the Universe'. And that's what this book is.

It's a pleasure and a privilege to embark on this journey with you. If you're a reader of ours already, thank you! And if you're not – jump on board the spaceship and prepare for lift off! Good luck on all your cosmic adventures and remember: don't fly too close to a black hole . . .

Lucy Hawking

Part One

In the Beginning

The Creation of the Universe

Professor STEPHEN HAWKING

There are many different stories about how the world started off. For example, according to the Bushongo people of central Africa, in the beginning there was only darkness, water and the great god Bumba. One day Bumba, in pain from a stomach ache, vomited up the Sun. The Sun dried up some of the water, leaving land. Still in pain, Bumba vomited up the Moon, the stars and then some animals – the leopard, the crocodile, the turtle and finally man.

Other peoples have other stories. They were early attempts to answer the Big Questions:

. Why are we here?

. Where did we come from?

The first scientific evidence to answer these questions was discovered about a century ago. It was found that other galaxies are moving away from us. The Universe is expanding; galaxies are getting further apart. This means that galaxies were closer together in the past. Nearly 14 billion years ago, the Universe would have been in a very hot and dense state. The moment it started to move apart is called the Big Bang.

The Universe started off with the Big Bang expanding faster and faster. This is called *inflation*, which also describes the way in which prices in the shops can go up and up. Inflation in the early Universe was much more rapid than inflation in prices: we think inflation is high if prices double in a year, but the Universe doubled in size many times in a tiny fraction of a second.

Inflation made the Universe very large and very smooth and flat. But it wasn't completely smooth: there were tiny variations in the Universe from place to place. These variations caused minute differences in the temperature of the early Universe, which we can see in what is known as the cosmic microwave background. The variations mean that some regions will be expanding slightly slower. The slower regions will eventually stop expanding and collapse to form galaxies and stars. We owe our existence to these variations. If the early Universe had been completely smooth, there would be no galaxies or stars and so life couldn't have developed.

The Big Bang

The Big Bang is a theory – an idea or a group of ideas – about how the Universe began. Scientists look for evidence to show that their ideas are correct. Most scientists accept the Big Bang theory.

A Voyage Across the Universe

Professor BERNARD CARR

School of Physics and Astronomy,
Queen Mary University of London

Before setting out we must understand what we mean by the terms 'voyage' and 'Universe'. The word 'Universe' literally means everything that exists. However, the history of astronomy might be regarded as a sequence of steps, and at each step the Universe has appeared to get bigger. So what we mean by 'everything' has changed over time.

Nowadays most cosmologists accept the Big Bang theory – according to which the Universe started in a state of great compression around 14 billion years ago. This means that the furthest we can see is the distance that light has travelled since the Big Bang. This defines the size of the observable Universe.

5

So what is meant by a 'voyage'? First we must distinguish between peering across the Universe and travelling across it. Peering is what astronomers do and, as we will see, involves looking back in time. Travelling is what astronauts do and involves crossing space. Travelling can also involve another kind of voyage. For as we travel from the Earth to the edge of the observable Universe, we are essentially retracing the history of human thought about the scale of the Universe. We will now discuss these three journeys in turn.

The voyage back through time

The information astronomers receive comes from electromagnetic waves that travel at the speed of light (300,000 km/ 186,000 miles per second). This is very fast but it is finite and astronomers often measure distance by the equivalent light travel time. Light takes several minutes to reach us from the Sun, for instance, but years from the nearest star, millions of years from the nearest big galaxy (Andromeda) and many billions of years from the most distant galaxies.

This means that as one peers across greater distances, one is also looking further into the past. For example, if we observe a galaxy 10 million light years away, we are seeing it as it was 10 million years ago. A voyage across the Universe in this sense is therefore not only a journey through space; it is also a journey back through time – right back to the Big Bang itself.

We cannot actually observe all the way back to the Big Bang. The early Universe was so hot that it formed a fog of particles that we cannot see through. As the Universe expanded, it cooled and about 380,000 years after the Big Bang the fog lifted. However, we can still use our theories to speculate about what the Universe was like before then. Since the density and temperature increase as we go back in time, our speculation depends on our theories in an area called high energy physics, but we now have a fairly complete picture of the history of the Universe.

One might expect that our voyage back through time would end at the Big Bang. However, scientists are now trying to understand the physics of creation itself, and any mechanism that can produce our Universe could in principle generate others. For example, some people believe the Universe undergoes cycles of expansion and collapse, giving us universes strung out in time. Others think that our Universe is just one of many 'bubbles' spread out in space. These are variants of what is called the 'multiverse' proposal.

The voyage across space

Travelling across the Universe physically is much more challenging because of the time it would take. The physicist Albert Einstein proposed two important theories about space and time. In his special theory of relativity (1905) he suggests that no spaceship could travel faster than the speed of light. This means it would take at least 100,000 years to cross the Galaxy and 10 billion years to cross the Universe – at least as judged by someone who stays on Earth. But special relativity also predicts that time flows more slowly for moving observers, so the trip could be much quicker for the astronauts themselves. Indeed, if one could travel at the speed of light, no time at all would pass!

No spaceship can travel as fast as light, but one could still gradually accelerate towards this maximum speed; the time experienced would then be much shorter than that on Earth. For example, if one were propelled with the acceleration with which bodies fall due to gravity on Earth, a journey across our Milky Way Galaxy would only seem to take about 30 years. One could therefore return to Earth in one's *own* lifetime, although one's friends would have died long ago. If one continued to accelerate beyond the Galaxy for a century, one could, in principle, travel to the edge of the currently observable Universe!

Einstein's other theory, the general theory of relativity (1915) could allow even more exotic possibilities. For example, maybe astronauts could one day use wormholes or space warp effects – just like in *Star Trek* and other popular science fiction series – to make these journeys even faster and get home again without losing any friends. But this is all very speculative.

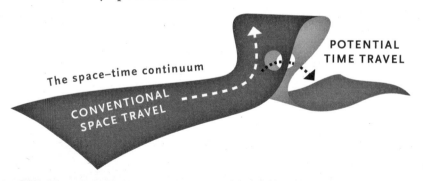

The space–time continuum

CONVENTIONAL SPACE TRAVEL

POTENTIAL TIME TRAVEL

The voyage through the history of human thought about the Universe

To the ancient Greeks, the Earth was the centre of the Universe, with the planets, the Sun and the stars being relatively close. This geocentric view (*geos* = Earth) was demolished in the sixteenth century, when Copernicus showed that the Earth and other planets move round the Sun (*helios*). However, this heliocentric picture did not last very long. Several decades later, Galileo used his newly invented telescope to show that the Milky Way – then known only as a band of light in the sky – consists of numerous stars like the Sun. This discovery not only diminished the status of the Sun, it also vastly increased the size of the known Universe.

By the eighteenth century it was accepted that the Milky Way is a disc of stars (the Galaxy) held together by gravity. However, most astronomers still assumed that the Milky Way comprised the whole Universe and this galactocentric view persisted well into the twentieth century. Then, in 1924, Edwin Hubble measured the distance to our nearest neighbouring big galaxy (Andromeda) and showed that it had to be well outside the Milky Way. Another shift in the size of the Universe!

Within a few more years Hubble had obtained data on several dozen nearby galaxies. His data showed that the galaxies are all moving away from us at a speed that is proportional to their distances from us. The easiest way to picture this is to think of space itself as expanding, just like the surface of an inflating balloon on to which the galaxies are painted. This expansion is known as Hubble's Law, and it has now been shown to apply up to distances of tens of billions of light years, a region containing hundreds of billions of galaxies. Yet another huge shift of scale!

The cosmocentric (cosmos = universe) view regards this as the final shift in the size of the Universe. This is because the cosmic expansion means that, as one goes back in time, the galaxies get closer together and eventually merge. Before that, the density just continues to increase – back to the Big Bang 14 billion years ago – and we can never see beyond the distance travelled by light since then. However, recently there has been an interesting observational development. Although one expects the expansion of the Universe to slow down because of gravity, current observations suggest that it is actually accelerating. Theories to explain this suggest that our observable Universe could be a part of a much larger 'bubble'. And this bubble could itself be just one of many bubbles!

What next?

So the endpoint of all three of our journeys – the first back through time, the second across space, and the third retracing the history of human thought – is the same: those unobservable universes which can only be glimpsed through theories and visited in our minds!

Albert Einstein
(1879—1955)

Albert Einstein, a physicist and mathematician, was born in Germany, but his family then moved to Italy, then to Switzerland. He showed an interest in science from an early age – at 5 he was fascinated by a compass, and the way the needle kept pointing in the same direction. At the age of 12, he taught himself algebra and geometry.

In 1905, when he was 26, he published three papers about science. One of them, 'On the Electrodynamics of Moving Bodies', is better known as 'the special theory of relativity'. Ten years later, in 1915, he produced his 'general theory of relativity'.

Einstein was Jewish, and in December 1932, a month before Adolf Hitler became Chancellor of Germany, Einstein gave up his German citizenship. He moved to the USA, where he lived for the rest of his life. He was a pacifist, and he was opposed to the atom bomb. He wanted peace among all nations and a world government.

Albert Einstein was awarded the Nobel Prize in Physics in 1921. He is considered by many as the greatest mathematical physicist of all time.

Einstein's Theories

The Theory of Special Relativity

Everything in the Universe is moving. Relativity describes the links between space, time and movement. In his theory of special relativity, Einstein proposed that the speed of light in a vacuum will be the same for any observer, however much the source of light may be moving. Also, the laws of physics are the same for all observers if they are in uniform motion relative to one another. This theory produces some interesting results, including the facts that energy and mass are interchangeable and that nothing can travel faster than light. From this theory comes Einstein's famous theorem:

$$E = mc^2$$

The Theory of General Relativity

This is about gravity. Einstein argued that matter in space distorts the space around it – it curves it. The curving is what we think of as gravity, but the sort of geometry we normally use only works on things that are flat, so can't be used to describe curved space. General relativity describes how gravity affects time as well as space.

Uniformity in Space

In order to apply general relativity to the Universe as a whole, we usually make some assumptions:

- Every location in space should behave in the same way (homogeneity).
- Every direction in space should look the same (isotropy).

This leads to a picture of the Universe which:

- is uniform in space
- starts with a Big Bang
- and then expands equally everywhere.

This picture is strongly supported by astronomical observations – what we can see in space through telescopes on the ground and in space.

Yet the Universe can't be exactly uniform in space, because this would mean that structures like galaxies, stars, solar systems, planets and people couldn't exist. A pattern of tiny ripples over the uniformity is needed to explain how the first patches of gas and dark matter could begin to collapse, so that the laws of physics could go on to create stars and planets.

Find out more about dark matter on pages 20 and 191.

Because the gas and dark matter start out nearly uniform, and because we believe the same laws of physics apply everywhere, we expect that all galaxies form in a similar way. So distant galaxies should have similar types of stars, planets, asteroids and comets to those that we can see in our own Milky Way.

Where the initial tiny ripples came from is not yet completely understood. The best theory at the moment is that they came from microscopic quantum jitters that were magnified by a very rapid early expansion phase – called inflation – which took place during a very tiny fraction of the first second after the Big Bang.

Edwin Hubble
(1889—1953)

Edwin Hubble was an American astronomer. At school, he was a star athlete and had good grades in all subjects except spelling. As an astronomer he worked in California, at the Mount Wilson Observatory. In 1923, using the enormous 2.5m (100-inch) Hooker Telescope, he gazed at the Andromeda Nebula. He found a special kind of star called a Cepheid variable star that allowed him to work out that the Andromeda Nebula was 900,000 light years from Earth. It could not possibly be in our Milky Way Galaxy because our Galaxy's radius is 52,850 light years – meaning the Andromeda Nebula was actually the Andromeda Galaxy. This was the first time another galaxy had been found and suggested the Universe was composed of many more, some of which Hubble later found. He also worked out a way of classifying galaxies by their shape, and that the further away a galaxy was from the Solar System, the faster it would be travelling.

It's since been calculated that Andromeda is 2 million light years away, but nevertheless what Hubble discovered was groundbreaking and proved that Andromeda was outside our Galaxy.

The Theory of Everything

Throughout history, people have looked around and tried to understand the amazing things they saw, asking:

. **What are these objects?**

. **Why do they move and change like that?**

. **Were they always there?**

. **What do they tell us about why we're here?**

Only in the last few centuries have we started to find scientific answers.

Classical Theory

In 1687 Isaac Newton, the great English mathematician and physicist, published his Laws of Motion, describing how forces change the way objects move, and the Law of Universal Gravitation, which says that every object in the Universe attracts every other object with a force – *gravity* – which is why we are stuck to the Earth's surface, why the Earth orbits the Sun, and how planets and stars were created. On the scale of planets, stars and galaxies, gravity is the architect controlling the grand structure of the Universe. Newton's laws are still good enough to place satellites in orbit and send spacecraft to other planets. But more modern theories, including Einstein's theories of relativity, are needed when objects are very fast, or very massive, and yet another theory is needed to explain the behaviour of very tiny things such as atoms and particles.

The Laws of Motion

1. Every particle remains at rest, or in motion along a straight line with constant velocity, unless acted on by an external force.

2. The rate of change of momentum of a particle is equal in magnitude to the external force, and in the same direction as the force.

3. If a particle exerts a force on a second particle, then the second particle exerts an equal but opposite force on the first particle.

The Law of Universal Gravitation

Every particle in the Universe attracts every other particle with a force, pointing along the line between the particles, which is directly proportional to the product of their masses and inversely proportional to the square of the distance between them.

Sir Isaac Newton
(1642—1727)

Isaac Newton was an English mathematician and physicist. His father died when he was a child and he was brought up by his grandmother. When he was at school he enjoyed making sundials and water clocks. There is a famous story that he saw an apple fall off a tree in an orchard at home and he was inspired to work out the laws of gravity. He had certainly worked out almost all of the universal laws of gravitation by the time he was 23.

Newton also found that white light could be split into colours using a prism. He invented a new kind of telescope. Although he was well known among the scientists and mathematicians of his day, he did not publish his work until quite late in his life. He was twice MP for Cambridge University, and he was knighted in 1705.

Quantum Theory

Classical theories are fine for big things, like galaxies, cars or even bacteria. But they can't explain how atoms work – in fact, they say atoms can't exist! In the early twentieth century, physicists realized they needed to develop a completely new theory to account for the properties of very small things like atoms or parts of atoms, such as electrons. This is quantum theory. The version that sums up our current knowledge of fundamental particles and forces is known as the Standard Model. It has quarks and leptons (the component particles of matter), force particles (the gluon, photon, W and Z), and the Higgs boson (which is needed to explain part of the masses of the other particles). Many scientists think this is too complicated, and would like a simpler model.

Also, where is the dark matter astronomers have discovered? And what about gravity? The force particle for gravity is called the graviton, but adding it to the Standard Model is difficult because gravity is very different – it changes the shape of space–time.

A theory explaining *all* the forces and *all* the particles – a Theory of Everything – might look very different to anything we have seen before, because it would need to explain space–time as well as gravity. But if it exists, it should explain the physical workings of the whole Universe, including the heart of black holes, the Big Bang and the far future of the cosmos. Finding it would be a spectacular achievement.

Dark Matter

Dark matter is an idea. The Universe behaves in a way that cannot be explained by the amount of material we can see. A galaxy would have to be about ten times bigger than the galaxy we can see to explain its behaviour. Scientists don't know what else might be present – they can't see anything – so they call the missing part dark matter. It could be particles, or very small dim stars, or black holes – some scientists think dark matter could be hot, and some think it could be cold. Discussions – and research – continue.

Max Planck
(1858—1947)

Max Planck was a German mathematical physicist. He could have been a musician – he was a good singer, and he played the piano, organ and cello well – but he decided to be a scientist instead. He was interested in thermodynamics – how objects take in, or absorb, heat energy, and give it out, or emit it. In his quantum theory, which came out in 1900, Planck proposed that energy was absorbed or emitted in small bursts, called quanta. In 1905, Planck's work led Albert Einstein to independently produce a similar theory about light. Max Planck won the Nobel Prize in Physics in 1918.

The Big Bang

Imagine that you are sitting inside the Universe at this very early time (obviously, you couldn't sit outside it). You would have to be very tough because the temperatures and pressures inside this Big Bang soup are so tremendously high. Back then, all the matter that we see around us today was squeezed into a region much smaller than an atom.

It's a tiny fraction of a second after the Big Bang, and everything looks much the same in all directions. There is no fireball racing outwards; instead, there is a hot blob of material, filling all of space.

What is this material? We aren't certain – it may be particles of a type we don't see today; it may even be little loops of 'string'; but it will definitely be 'exotic' stuff that we couldn't expect to see now, even in our largest particle accelerators.

Find out about particle accelerators on page 91.

When the Big Bang occurs, this blob of very hot exotic matter is expanding as the space it fills grows bigger – matter in all directions is streaming away from you, and the blob is becoming less dense. The further away the matter is, the more space is expanding between you and it, so the faster the matter moves away.

The furthest material is actually moving away from you faster than the speed of light!

A lot of complicated changes now happen very fast – all in the first second after the Big Bang. The expansion of the tiny Universe allows the hot exotic fluid to cool. This causes sudden changes, like when water changes as it cools to form ice.

The early Universe is still much smaller than an atom. One of the changes in the fluid causes a stupendous increase in the speed of expansion (inflation). The size of the Universe doubles, then doubles again, and again, and so on until it has doubled in size around 90 times, increasing from subatomic to human scale. Like pulling a bedspread straight, this enormous stretching flattens out any big bumps in the material so that the Universe we eventually see will be very smooth and almost the same in all directions.

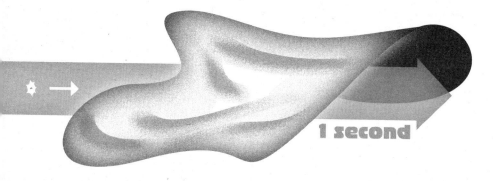

1 second

On the other hand, microscopic ripples in the fluid are also stretched and made much bigger, and these will trigger the formation of stars and galaxies later.

Inflation ends abruptly and releases a large amount of energy, which creates a wash of new particles. The exotic matter has disappeared and been replaced by more familiar particles – including quarks (the building blocks of protons and neutrons, although it is still too hot for these to form), antiquarks, gluons (which fly between both quarks and antiquarks), photons (the particles light is made of), electrons and other particles well known to physicists. There may also be particles of dark matter, but although it seems these have to appear, we don't yet understand what they are.

Where did the exotic matter go? Some of it was hurled away from us during inflation, to regions of the Universe we may never see; some of it decayed into less exotic particles as the temperature fell. The material all around us is much less hot and dense than it was, though still much hotter and denser than anywhere today (including inside stars). The Universe is filled with a hot, luminous fog (known as plasma) made mainly from quarks, antiquarks and gluons.

Expansion continues (at a much slower rate than during inflation), and eventually the temperature falls enough for the quarks and antiquarks to bind together in groups of two or three, forming protons, neutrons and other particles, including a type known as hadrons. Still little can be seen through the luminous foggy plasma as the Universe reaches one second old.

Over the next few seconds, there are fireworks as most of the matter and antimatter produced so far annihilate each other, producing floods of new photons. The fog is now mainly protons, neutrons, electrons, dark matter and (most of all) photons, but the charged protons and electrons stop the photons travelling very far, so visibility in this expanding and cooling fog is still very poor.

When two particles with different numbers of electrons start reacting to each other, something called an ionic bond is formed, and the particle becomes charged – either positively or negatively.

Antimatter

In antimatter, particles are the same as those that make up ordinary matter, but everything about them, including their electric charge, is reversed. If ordinary matter and antimatter meet, they destroy each other.

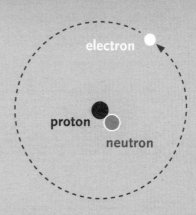

electron

proton

neutron

HYDROGEN ATOM

When the Universe is a few minutes old, the surviving protons and the neutrons combine to form atomic nuclei, mainly of what will become hydrogen and helium. These are still charged, so the fog remains impossible to see through. At this point, the foggy material is not unlike what you would find inside a star today, but of course it fills the whole Universe.

After the frantic action of the first few minutes of existence, the Universe stays much the same for the next few hundred thousand years, continuing to expand and cool down, the hot fog becoming steadily thinner, dimmer and redder as the wavelengths of light are stretched by the expansion of space.

Then, after 380,000 years, when the part of the Universe that we will eventually see from Earth has grown to be millions of light years across, the fog finally clears – electrons are captured by the hydrogen and helium nuclei to form whole atoms. Because the electric charges of the electrons and nuclei cancel each other out, the complete atoms are not charged, so the photons can now travel uninterrupted – the Universe has become transparent.

After this long wait in the fog, what do you see? Only a fading red glow in all directions, which becomes redder and dimmer as the expansion of space continues to stretch the wavelengths of the photons. Finally, the light ceases to be visible at all and there is only darkness everywhere – we have entered the Cosmic Dark Ages.

The photons from that last glow have been travelling

through the Universe ever since, steadily becoming even redder – today they can be detected as what is called cosmic microwave background (CMB) radiation, and they are still arriving on Earth from every direction in the sky.

The Universe's Dark Ages last for a few hundred million years, during which time there is literally nothing to see. The Universe is still filled with matter, but almost all of it is dark matter, and the rest is hydrogen and helium gas, and none of this produces any new light. In the darkness, however, there are quiet changes.

The microscopic ripples, which were magnified by inflation, have meant that some regions contain slightly more mass than average. This increases the pull of gravity towards those regions, bringing even more mass in, and the dark matter, hydrogen gas and helium gas already there are pulled closer together. Slowly, over millions of years, dense patches of dark matter and gas gather as a result of this increased gravity, growing gradually by pulling in more matter, and more rapidly by colliding and merging with other patches. As the gas falls into these patches, the atoms speed up and become hotter. Every now and then, the gas becomes hot enough to stop collapsing, unless it can cool down by emitting photons, or is compressed by collision with another cloud of matter.

If the gas cloud collapses enough, it breaks into spherical blobs so dense that the heat inside can no longer get out – finally, a point is reached when hydrogen nuclei in the cores of the blobs are so hot and squashed together that they start to fuse (meaning that they merge) into nuclei of helium and release nuclear energy. You are sitting inside one of these collapsing patches of dark matter and gas (because this is where the Earth's Galaxy will be one day), and you may be surprised when the darkness around you is broken by the first of these nearby blobs bursting into bright light – these are the first stars to be born, and the Dark Ages are over.

The first stars burn their hydrogen quickly, and in their final stages they fuse together whatever nuclei they can find to create heavier atoms than helium: carbon, nitrogen, oxygen and the other heavier types of atom which are all around us (and *in* us) today. These atoms are scattered like ashes back into the nearby gas clouds in great explosions and get swept up in the creation of the next generation of stars. The process continues – new stars form from the accumulating gas and ash, die and create more ash. As younger stars are created, the familiar spiral shape of our Galaxy – the Milky Way – takes form. The same thing is happening in similar patches of dark matter and gas peppered across the visible Universe.

The Sun

Nine billion years have passed since the Big Bang, and now a young star surrounded by planets, built from hydrogen and helium gas and the ash from dead stars, takes shape and ignites.

In another 4.5 billion years the third planet out from this star could still be the only place in the known Universe where human beings can comfortably exist. They – you – will see stars, clouds of gas and dust, galaxies and cosmic microwave background radiation everywhere in the sky – but not the dark matter, which is most of what lies there. Neither will you be able to see anything of those parts that are so distant that even the CMB photons from there have yet to arrive. Indeed there may be parts of the Universe from which light will never reach our planet at all.

The Expansion of the Universe

The astronomer Edwin Hubble used the 2.5m (100-inch) telescope on Mount Wilson, California, to study the night sky. He found that some of the nebulae – fuzzy, luminous specks in the night sky – are in fact galaxies, like our Milky Way (although the galaxies could be of widely varying sizes), each containing billions and billions of stars. And he discovered a remarkable fact: other galaxies appear to be moving away from us, and the further they are from us, the faster their apparent speed. Suddenly humanity's Universe became much, much larger.

The Universe is still expanding: distances between galaxies are increasing with time. Think again of the Universe as the surface of a balloon on which one has painted blobs to represent galaxies. If one blows up the balloon, the blobs or galaxies move away from each other; the further apart they are, the faster the distance between them increases.

The Red Shift

Very hot objects in space, like stars, produce visible light, but as the Universe is constantly expanding, these distant stars and their home galaxies are moving away from Earth. This stretches their light as it travels through space towards us – the further it travels, the more stretched it becomes. The stretching makes visible light look redder – which is known as the cosmological red shift.

The Early Atmosphere

+ The Earth's atmosphere hasn't always been as it is today. Were we to travel back 3.5 billion years (to when the Earth was about 1 billion years old), we would not be able to breathe.

+ The atmosphere 3.5 billion years ago contained no oxygen. It was mostly made of nitrogen, hydrogen, carbon dioxide and methane, but the exact composition is not known. What is known, however, is that huge volcanic eruptions occurred around that period, releasing steam, carbon dioxide, ammonia and hydrogen sulphide into the atmosphere. Hydrogen sulphide smells like rotten eggs and is poisonous when encountered in large amounts.

+ Today, our atmosphere is made of approximately 78% nitrogen, 21% oxygen and 0.93% argon. The remaining 0.07% is mostly carbon dioxide (0.04%) and a mixture of neon, helium, methane, krypton and hydrogen.

Did Life Come from Mars?

Dr BRANDON CARTER

Laboratoire de l'Univers et de ses Théories,
l'Observatoire de Paris-Meudon, France

Where and when did life as we know it begin? Did it begin on Earth? Or could it have come from Mars?

A couple of centuries ago, most people believed that humans and other species had been present since the creation of the Earth. The Earth was thought to be, essentially, the whole of the material world, and the creation was described as a rather sudden event, like the Big Bang that the majority of scientists believe in today. This was taught in creation stories, like the one in Genesis, the first book of the Bible, and other cultures throughout the world have similar stories of a one-off moment of creation.

Although some astronomers did think about the vastness of space, its study only really began after Galileo (1564–1642) made one of the first-ever telescopes. His discoveries showed that the Universe contained many other worlds – some of which could, like our own planet, be inhabited. The immensity of the Universe – and the evidence that its

creation must have happened long before our own species arrived on the scene – did not begin to be generally recognized until much later on, in what is known as the Age of Enlightenment. This was the eighteenth-century period in which there were many inventions, such as the hydrogen balloon, and particularly the steam engine. These inventions triggered the technological and industrial revolution of the nineteenth century. During that innovative time, the study of rock formation by sedimentation in shallow seas led geologists to understand that such processes must have been going on not just for thousands or even millions of years, but for thousands of millions of years – what we now call gigayears.

Modern humans appear to have arrived in the rest of the world from Africa 50,000 years ago, but modern archaeology has shown quite clearly that it was only about 6,000 years ago that early human societies began to develop what we call civilization – economic systems with the exchange of different kinds of goods. A very important factor in any civilization is the exchange not just of goods but of information. But how was this information stored or spread? Suitable recording mechanisms were needed.

Modern geophysicists now believe that Planet Earth, and our Solar System, was formed about 4.5 to 4.6 gigayears ago, when the Universe – now aged about 14 gigayears – was just over 9 gigayears old.

Scratching a Stone

Before the invention of paper and ink, one of the earliest methods humans used to record information was marks scratched on clay tablets – the distant ancestors of modern computer memory chips. This sharing and collecting of knowledge, particularly the kind we now call scientific, became an objective in its own right.

The relatively recent development of civilization depended, of course, on the emergence of what has been called intelligent life: beings with a sufficient sense of self-awareness to recognize themselves in a mirror. There are several known examples on our own planet: elephants and dolphins, as well as anthropoids – the group that includes chimpanzees and other apes, Neanderthals, and modern human beings like us. So far, no signs of intelligent life have been detected elsewhere in the Universe.

1,000,000,000 years = 1 gigayear

How did these intelligent life forms on Earth come into being?

Fossil remains had suggested the idea that modern plants and animals could have arisen from other life forms present on Earth in earlier times, but people couldn't understand how the various species could be so well adapted without having been designed in advance. The idea of continuous evolution became generally accepted only after Charles Darwin, in his book *On the Origin of Species* (published in 1859) explained the principle of adaptation by a process he called natural selection. Understanding how this actually works, however, only became possible much more recently (in the late 1950s), when we discovered DNA.

This modern DNA-based understanding of the evolutionary process is supported by the fossil record – as far as

Turn to page 50 to find out more about Charles Darwin's theory of natural selection.

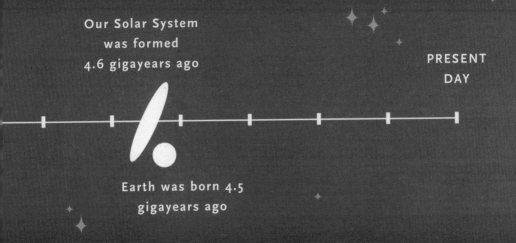

Our Solar System
was formed
4.6 gigayears ago

PRESENT
DAY

Earth was born 4.5
gigayears ago

it goes. The trouble is that the record does not go very far back – less than a gigayear, which is only a fraction of the total age of the Earth.

Early, simple life forms developed before what is known in geology as the Cambrian era. This was a period of about 53 million years, and it was the first time period in what is known as the Paleozoic era. We can see fairly clearly how (though not precisely why) what we should recognize as intelligent life forms evolved from early life forms over the last 500 million years. But there is no proper record of how the pre-Cambrian life forms evolved in the first place.

One problem is that it is only since the Cambrian era that large bony animals, which easily turn into fossils, have been present. Their largest predecessors are believed to have been soft-bodied creatures (like modern jellyfish); further back in time the only life forms seem to have been microscopic single-celled creatures. These don't leave clear fossil records.

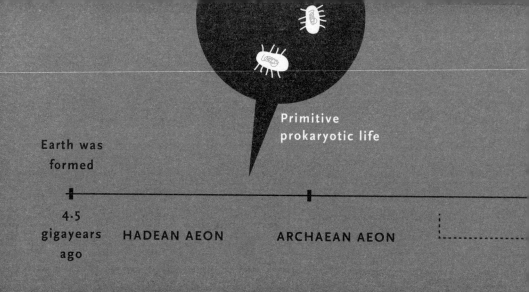

Earth was
formed

Primitive
prokaryotic life

4.5
gigayears   HADEAN AEON   ARCHAEAN AEON
ago

Going back even further, it is evident that evolution must have been very slow. And tricky to achieve. Even if environmentally favourable planets were fairly common in the Universe, the odds against the evolution of advanced life on any single planet would have been very high. This means that it would only occur on a very small fraction of them. The planet on which we find ourselves must be one of those rare exceptions. And it could still have easily gone wrong. There is a calculation by astrophysicists known as the solar-age coincidence. This shows that, in the time taken by evolution on Earth to lead to intelligent life, a large part of the hydrogen fuel reserves powering our Sun were used up.

If our evolution had been just a little bit slower we would never have got here at all before the Sun burned itself out!

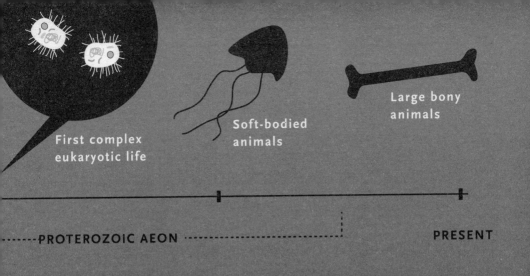

First complex
eukaryotic life

Soft-bodied
animals

Large bony
animals

PROTEROZOIC AEON   PRESENT

So which of the essential evolutionary steps would be the
hardest to achieve in the available time?

One difficult step on Earth may have been the beginning
of what is known as eukaryotic life – in which cells have an
elaborate structure with nuclei and ribosomes. Eukaryotes
include large multi-cellular animals like us, as well as
single-celled species like the amoeba. The fossil record
shows that the first eukaryotic life appeared on Earth at the
beginning of the Proterozoic aeon, about 2 gigayears ago,
when the Earth was only about half its present age. Before
this period, more primitive prokaryotic life forms, such as
bacteria (with cells that are too small to contain nuclei), are
now thought to have been widespread. This was in what is
known as the Archaean aeon, which began when the Earth
was less than 1 gigayear old.

There is evidence for the existence of this kind of
primitive life right back at the very beginning of the

Archaean aeon – so we are now faced with a puzzle, because this implies that the whole process by which life actually originated must have occurred during the preceding epoch. The era before the Archaean is known as the Hadean aeon – the earliest aeon of the Earth's history.

Why should this be a problem? Well, the Hadean aeon was certainly long enough – nearly a gigayear – but conditions on Earth at that time would have been literally infernal, as the name suggests ('Hades' is the ancient Greek version of hell). This was when debris left over from the formation of the Solar System was crashing into the Moon and forming craters there. And the Earth, with its greater mass and gravitational attraction, would at that time have been subject to even heavier cratering. This bombardment would have caused frequent reheating of our planetary environment. Life forms just beginning to develop could hardly have avoided being nipped in the bud.

The planet Mars, however, has a lesser mass and is further away from the Sun, so it has recently been proposed that the bombardment of Mars could have become less intense sooner than that of the Earth. Chunks of debris may also have been frequently knocked off Mars and in some cases subsequently swept up by the Earth. This would mean that life may have originated on Mars – before it could have survived here.

Analysis by electron microscope of a meteorite that did

reach Earth from Mars (meteorite ALH84001) has shown structures resembling fossil microbes. This proves that fossil organisms may have reached the Earth from Mars. But that would still not account for life then appearing here unless living – not just fossil – organisms could survive the necessary migration by meteor. This is a question that is currently being very hotly debated.

An even more interesting question is whether the environment on Mars at that time (in what is known as the Phyllocian period, roughly coinciding with the Hadean era on the Earth) really would have been suitable for primitive life.

Conditions on Mars nowadays are clearly unfavourable, at least on the surface – a cold dry desert with hardly any atmosphere except for a little carbon dioxide. Probes landing on Mars have, however, confirmed that there is a considerable amount of frozen water at the poles. Additionally, there are many observable features of the kind expected from erosion by rivers or by surf at a seashore. This means that at some stage in the Martian past there must have been a large amount of liquid water present – exactly what is needed for our kind of life to begin. During that early period the water would have formed an ocean. Initially this could have been several thousand metres (or feet) deep with its centre near what is now the Martian north pole.

So life could have originated at the edge of this ocean, way back in Martian history.

Objections

There are a couple of objections to this theory. One is that the atmosphere would not have contained oxygen. However, primitive life forms on Earth are believed to have been able to survive in an atmosphere that was also very deficient in oxygen so that might not have mattered.

Another objection is that the ancient Martian ocean would have been too salty for known terrestrial life forms. But maybe Martian life was originally adapted to very salty conditions, or perhaps it developed in freshwater lakes?

Thus life may well have begun on Mars – at the edge of a huge ocean there – then hitched a ride to the Earth on board a meteor. So our ultimate ancestors may, in fact, have been Martians!

Galileo Galilei
(1564–1642)

Galileo was an Italian mathematician, physicist and astronomer. He was born near Pisa, Italy, though his family came from Florence. At first he studied medicine, then switched to mathematics and philosophy. When he was 18, he noticed that a candelabrum in Pisa cathedral was swinging, and that each swing took the same time whatever distance it travelled. This allowed him to improve pendulums in clocks. One story tells how he dropped stones from the Leaning Tower of Pisa and discovered their velocity (the speed of their fall in a straight line) was the same whatever the size and weight of the stone. Galileo invented an early thermometer, and he improved on a Dutch invention to produce a telescope that could magnify objects by a power of 32. With this he made many important astronomical observations and discoveries.

James Watson
(1928—)
and
Francis Crick
(1916—2004)

The American scientist James Watson and the
British scientist Francis Crick were biologists who
worked together at the Cavendish Laboratory
in Cambridge. They were interested in DNA, a
material that contains hereditary information that
is passed on in the cells of a living organism.
They used the work of Maurice Wilkins and
Rosalind Franklin to help in their research, which
resulted in the discovery that the structure of
DNA is a double helix. Watson, Crick and Wilkins
together received the Nobel Prize in Physiology
or Medicine in 1962. Sadly, Rosalind Franklin had
died in 1958, and wasn't included in the prize,
even though her work on DNA was crucial.

How Did Life Begin?

Miller and Urey's Experiment

In 1953 two American scientists named Stanley Miller and Harold Urey were working on the origin of life on Earth. They believed the ingredients for life could appear out of completely natural phenomena in the Earth's early atmosphere.

At that time scientists had an idea about the kind of chemical compounds the early atmosphere probably contained. They also knew that lightning was frequent. So Miller and Urey conducted an experiment in which they stoked these chemical compounds with electric sparks (to mimic lightning). Astonishingly, they discovered that they had created special organic compounds.

Organic compounds are molecules that contain carbon and hydrogen. Some of these molecules, like the ones called amino acids, are necessary for life. Miller and Urey's experiment produced amino acids and gave hope to the scientific community that it may be possible to create life in a laboratory.

Today, however, more than 60 years after Miller and Urey, such a creation has yet to be achieved and we still do not know how life appeared on Earth. But we have been able to create, under special circumstances that mimic conditions on Earth a long time ago, more and more of the basic chemical building blocks of life.

Stanley Miller
(1930–2007)
and
Harold Urey
(1893–1981)

Stanley Miller was an American chemist who followed his brother to the University of California, Berkeley, and picked chemistry like his brother because he thought his brother would be able to help him. He received his doctorate in 1954, completed a one-year fellowship at the California Institute of Technology, went to Columbia University, New York City, for 5 years and then remained for the rest of his career at the University of California, San Diego.

Harold Urey was an American chemist who had won the Nobel Prize in Chemistry in 1934 for the discovery of deuterium, also called heavy hydrogen. He was also Director of War Research for the atomic bomb project at Columbia University.

Miller heard Urey give a lecture about the origins of the Solar System, and how very early life might have happened in such conditions. He was so inspired that he went to Urey to discuss a research project. After much persuasion, Urey agreed to work with Miller to investigate electrical discharges in gases, which gave insight into how amino acids could have come to be present on the early Earth. Miller wrote an account of his experiment for a scientific magazine and it was published within 3 months of being written because Urey asked *Science* to quickly review the manuscript and publish it as soon as possible.

The History of Life

Professor MICHAEL J. REISS

Institute of Education, University College London

When we look at the animals and plants around us, the sheer diversity of life seems amazing. Even in a busy city a single walk brings us into contact with dozens of species, from insects so small we can hardly see them, to trees and large animals like birds and mammals. In the countryside there are literally thousands of species in even a small bit of forest, grassland or marsh.

We still don't know how many species there are in the world. About 1.2 million have so far been carefully identified by scientists, described, classified and given a name – but the total figure is much bigger than that. The best current estimate is that there are about 8 or 9 million species in all, though some biologists think the figure could be much higher than this. This means that the great majority of species on our planet haven't even yet been given a name. They could go extinct and we wouldn't even notice!

Where do all these species come from? This is a question that humans have often asked. Many of the world's religions have an answer. They talk about God creating life. This answer isn't enough for scientists, though. Even if God did make species – including us – we want to know when and how!

It was Charles Darwin in the nineteenth century who provided the answer that we still think is correct.

Darwin realized that just as farmers can produce new breeds of farm animals by choosing to use only certain individuals to produce the next generation, so nature can produce new species by what he called 'natural selection'. Suppose, for example, that a widespread species of seed-eating bird occurs in some places where plants produce mainly small seeds and in some places where plants produce mainly large seeds. Suppose too that there is

Charles Darwin
(1809—1882)

Charles Darwin was the son of a well-known doctor. He studied medicine at Edinburgh, then decided he would train to become a clergyman while pursuing biology. Before he could take a job as a cleric, he was appointed as 'gentleman naturalist' to a naval survey ship, HMS *Beagle*, which was going to sail round the world – this allowed him to investigate plants, animals and geological formations in many different places. The voyage lasted from 1831–1836, and Darwin collected many specimens, and made many observations that influenced his thinking for the rest of his life.

Darwin was a wealthy man and was happily married. He and his wife, Emma, had servants and his wife ran the household. That gave Darwin time to do his scientific work, even though he and Emma had ten children, most of whom loved nothing more than to rush into their father's study and try to get him to play with them.

inevitably some variation in the size of the birds' beaks and that how large a bird's beak is partly depends on the size of its parents' beaks, so that birds with small beaks tend to produce offspring with small beaks and birds with large beaks produce offspring that typically also have large beaks.

Nothing very surprising, so far. But Darwin realized that if beak size is important for a bird's survival and reproduction – for example, because food is sometimes in short supply – then natural selection would gradually lead to changes in beak size. Over time, birds that live where the plants have large seeds would come to have large beaks, and birds that live where the plants have small seeds would evolve small beaks. Given enough time, the original single bird species might evolve into two new species, each one well adapted to its food source.

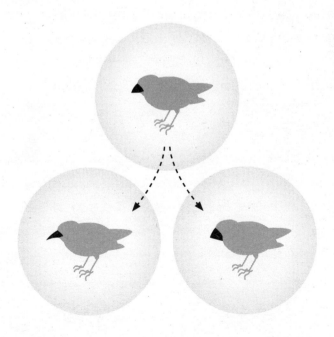

Darwin published his theory in 1859 in a book called *On the Origin of Species* (the full title is *On the Origin of Species by Means of Natural Selection, or the Preservation of Favoured Races in the Struggle for Life* – the Victorians liked long book titles). This is one of the most important scientific books ever written. It changed the way we see our world and has never been out of print. It is a long book but still very worth reading.

Darwin was the first to admit that his theory didn't explain everything. In particular, how did the first species come into existence? After all, his theory may explain how species can change over time and evolve into new species but it doesn't say anything about how the whole process gets going.

Darwin was a bit of a genius. Actually, he was more than a bit of a genius; he was a total genius. The tentative answer he came up with for the origin of the very first species is pretty much what many of today's scientists still think might be the case. On 1 February 1871 Darwin wrote to his close friend and fellow scientist Joseph Hooker:

> *It is often said that all the conditions for the first production of a living organism are now present, which could ever have been present.— But if (& oh what a big if) we could conceive in some warm little pond with all sorts of ammonia & phosphoric salts,—light,*

heat, electricity &c present, that a protein compound was chemically formed, ready to undergo still more complex changes, at the present day such matter wd be instantly devoured, or absorbed, which would not have been the case before living creatures were formed.

We still don't know for sure how life started. It might well have been in one or more of Darwin's 'warm little ponds', much as he suggested. But once it got going, there was no stopping life. As millions of years went by, life gradually reached more and more of the Earth's surface. Species got bigger and hardier.

They colonized the land and took to the air. Eventually, 3 to 4 billion years after the process started, we have whales and hummingbirds and giant redwood trees and beautiful orchids and all the other 8 or 9 million species there are today, including us.

And we are still discovering some of these species. Maybe you too might one day find yourself journeying to a part of our wonderful Earth and being the first person to identify a new species!

Genetics

Professor AMMAR AL CHALABI

Professor of Neurology and Complex Disease Genetics,
Maurice Wohl Clinical Neuroscience Institute

Do you have brown hair? Maybe it is black, ginger or blonde, or perhaps some other colour? You might have the same hair colour as someone else in your family. What about your tongue? Can you roll your tongue into a tube? Not everyone can, even if they try very hard. And your fingers – does anyone in your family have hair on the backs of their fingers? Some people do and some do not – you might need to look carefully to see it. So how does your body know what colour hair you should have, or whether you should be able to roll your tongue into a tube, or if it should put hair on the backs of your fingers? The answer is that all these things are controlled by instructions carried in every cell of your body, called genes. Genes tell your body how to make every part of itself, how to repair itself, how tall it should be, how many fingers it should have – in fact, almost anything you can think of, like a cookery book for making a person. You can think of each gene like a page in the cookery book, with a recipe for making a part of you.

The gene cookery book is a very big book. There are more than 20,000 pages, but that is because you are a very complicated thing to make!

We receive our genes from our parents. The pages in the cookery book for making you were copied from the pages in your parents' cookery books. Although everyone's cookery book has recipes for the same body parts, the recipes are not all exactly the same. For example, the recipe on the gene page for hair colour might say to use black or it might say to use ginger. If you have the black-hair recipe you will have black hair, and if you have the ginger-hair recipe you will have ginger hair. That is why we are all a little bit different, but we all look like humans. Sometimes, the gene recipe can be missing something important, or it might be changed in an important way. Imagine a recipe for strawberries and cream. If it said to use straw instead of strawberries, you probably would not want to eat it. If a big mistake like this happens in a gene recipe, it can cause problems and make people ill. On the other hand, if it said to use berries instead of strawberries, it might be fine, or it might be even better than the original.

What do genes look like? See if you can find some cotton thread. If you have very sharp eyesight, you might notice it is really two threads wound round each other very tightly. You can make this more obvious by trying to untwist it. A special twisted double thread like this, made of something called DNA, carries your genes. Now imagine the thread becoming bigger and bigger, until it is the size of a rope ladder. There are a lot of rungs on this ladder – 3 billion, in fact. That is so many that the ladder stretches to the Moon and back twice, or 40 times round the Earth. Remember, the ladder is your body's cookery book. It is so long because there are so many recipes.

Not all the rungs on the ladder are the same. There are four different types, and we name them with letters: G, A, T and C. Your body uses these four letters to write the words of the gene recipes, spelling them out on the ladder. So if you climb the ladder and the rungs read GATTCCCTGGACC, it might just look like some letters to you, but in fact it is a secret code. Your body can read the code easily and understand the words written on the ladder. We have only cracked a tiny bit of the genetic code. Even knowing that much is enough for doctors to be able to make new types of medicine.

Your body is made of trillions of cells. Each one

G

C

A

T

needs a copy of the gene recipes written on the very long rope ladder. Now, let's shrink the ladder back down until it is the size of a thread again, and then down still further, until it is so thin you cannot see it. Even at this scale, it is still 2 metres (6 ft) long! That is much too long to squeeze into a cell, so your body coils the tiny DNA ladder up very, very tightly. Now it fits! If you stretched out all the tiny DNA ladders in your body and laid them end to end, they would be twice as wide as the Solar System!

How does your body read a recipe from one of your genes? Microscopic machines unwind the bit of DNA ladder containing the gene recipe they need. The machines are not made by people. They are made by your body from gene recipes! The machines know how to read the genetic code, and they know what the order of letters means. They can follow the instructions on the DNA ladder and build all the different bits they need to make your body.

You are unique.

So, the book of recipes to make you is actually more than 20,000 genes, written in a genetic code, on a ladder called DNA, tightly coiled up and stored in each cell of your body, and your book of recipes is different from anyone else's in the whole world.

Part Two

What on Earth?

Earth: What's It Made Of?

Earth is the third-closest planet to the Sun.
Liquid water covers 70.8% of the surface of the Earth and the rest is divided into seven continents. These are: Asia (29.5% of the land surface of the Earth), Africa (20.5%), North America (16.5%), South America (12%), Antarctica (9%), Europe (7%) and Australia (5%). This definition of continents is mostly historical and cultural since, for instance, no expanse of water divides Asia from Europe. Geographically, there are only four continents that are not separated by water: Eurasia–Africa (57% of the land surface), the Americas (28.5%), Antarctica (9%) and Australia (5%). The remaining 0.5% is made up of islands, mostly scattered within Oceania in the central and south Pacific Ocean.

Earth's average distance to the Sun: 93 million miles (149.6 million km).

Sun

Mercury

Venus

Earth

Did you know?

A day on Earth is divided into 24 hours, but in fact it takes Earth 23 hours, 56 minutes and 4 seconds to rotate once on its axis. There is a discrepancy of 3 minutes and 56 seconds.

An Earth-year is the time it takes for the Earth to complete one revolution (or orbit) round the Sun. It may vary very slightly over time, but is around 365.25 days.

So far, the Earth is the only known planet in the Universe to harbour life.

North America

Europe

Asia

Africa

South America

Australia

Antarctica

How Long Is a 'Day' on Earth?

Why is a day in winter shorter than a day in summer?

It's because the Earth is tilted on its axis as it orbits the Sun. If the Earth stayed upright throughout its whole orbit, day and night would be exactly the same length every day of the year. But as it rotates, the Earth is at an angle of 23.5° to the Sun and this means that at one point in its orbit, the North Pole and the region we call the Arctic Circle are angled so far away from the Sun that they receive no daylight at all.

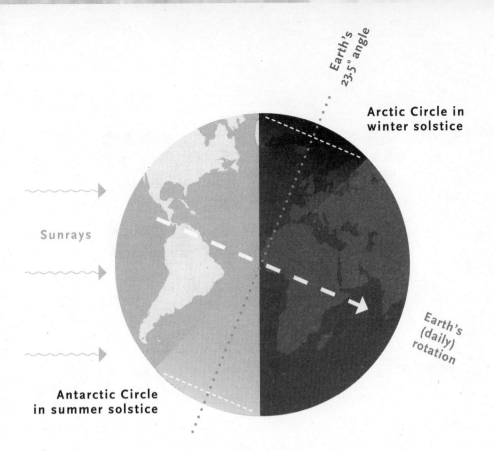

Earth's 23.5° angle

Arctic Circle in winter solstice

Sunrays

Antarctic Circle in summer solstice

Earth's (daily) rotation

In the northern hemisphere, this happens between 20 December and 23 December, otherwise known as the winter solstice.

At the same time, in the southern hemisphere, the South Pole is in full daylight for the whole 24-hour period.

As the Earth turns round the Sun, the tilt changes the area that receives sunlight until it is the other way round. At the summer solstice (between 20 June and 22 June), it is daylight for the full 24 hours at the North Pole, and it is completely dark at the South Pole. The rest of the world in between the poles receives a varying amount of light, lengthening or shortening the days.

The Goldilocks Zone

Do you remember the story of Goldilocks, the little girl who didn't like extremes? Too hard, too soft, too hot, too cold – these didn't suit her. She liked things to be just right.

Our planet, Earth, is 'just right'. We get light from the Sun, which heats us up – but not so much that the atmosphere burns away and the water evaporates, nor so little that Earth is a frozen desert in which no life can exist.

Water is liquid between 0°C (32°F), when it freezes, and 100°C (212°F), when it boils. Water is essential for life, because it can do so many things. It dissolves and mixes and spreads chemicals, allowing them to reform in many different ways, including as proteins and DNA, both building blocks of life.

There are four rocky planets orbiting our Sun – Mercury, Venus, Earth and Mars. Only Earth has liquid water and life – only Earth is in the Goldilocks Zone.

Scientists have found several thousand rocky planets orbiting stars in our Milky Way Galaxy, and they estimate that there are many more – at least 100 billion. They are very interested in planets in the 'Goldilocks Zone' – the distance from a planet's sun for the temperature on that planet to allow liquid water – and possibly life – to exist.

If you'd rather, you can call the area where the temperature of a planet orbiting a star would be 'just right' the Circumstellar Habitable Zone – CHZ – instead.

TOO WARM

The Oceans of Earth

Professor ROS E. M. RICKABY

Department of Earth Sciences, University of Oxford

arth – our blue planet – is exceptional in our Solar System as almost three quarters of its surface is covered by the oceans. But why are our oceans here? Intriguingly, Earth's oceans arrived from outer space. When the Earth was forming, it was too hot for water to condense on the planet. Just as tall mountains have snowy white tops above the 'snowline', where the cooling of the atmosphere with height allows snow to persist, so too there was a gradient of cooling to a snowline away from the ferociously hot early Sun.

Temperatures cold enough for ice grains to form were only reached further out in the Solar System, in the asteroid belt somewhere between Mars and Jupiter. Earth's oceans, therefore, had to be imported: many think this happened with a shower of comets or water-rich meteorites from the asteroid belt bombarding the early Earth.

Since then, these extraterrestrial water molecules have been neither created nor destroyed! For the subsequent 3.8 billion years (the first evidence for liquid water comes from sediments of this age found in southwest Greenland), our oceans have been trapped on the Earth's surface, where they go round in two cycles.

First, the warmth of the Sun in the tropics turns some of the ocean to water vapour (just like you see coming from a boiling kettle or a steam engine) which forms clouds. The vapour condenses into drops of water, creating rain, which falls and trickles across the land into streams and rivers before gushing back into the oceans.

Second, small amounts of water seep down into Earth's interior, through deep-sea trenches in the ocean crust. This water rapidly returns to the surface through volcanoes or hydrothermal vents.

You could be making a cup of tea out of water that was once slurped down by a thirsty T. Rex – and peed out again!

So the very same water molecules coming out of your taps at home have witnessed every second of Earth's history, from before the start of self-reproducing life itself to the emergence of multicelled organisms. Most probably, these water molecules passed through a dinosaur at some point.

Water, Water, Everywhere

What makes water so extraordinary, and the oceans so key to life, is its ability to dissolve things. Put some salt in a glass of water, or sugar in your tea, and those crystals will disappear, or dissolve. This is because of the slight charge or 'polarity' of water molecules, which attracts elements into solution.

A water molecule has two hydrogen atoms and one oxygen atom – chemists write this as H_2O. A hydrogen atom has a slight positive charge and an oxygen atom has a slight negative charge, but this is stronger than the charge of the hydrogen atoms. This means that each molecule of water has a positive end and a negative end. This is described as a 'polar molecule'.

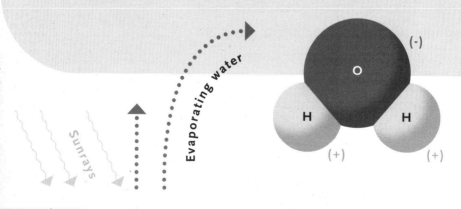

Sunrays

Evaporating water

(-)

O

H   H

(+)   (+)

Black smokers

THE OCEANS

Sediment

Water is even better at dissolving things if it is made a little acidic, by reacting with something like carbon dioxide to make carbonic acid. When the water cycle takes water from the oceans to clouds, then to rain and finally down rivers, water reacts with carbon dioxide in our atmosphere and becomes a little acidic. As a result, this carbonated rainwater dissolves elements out of the land (this is called erosion, or weathering), takes them into the rivers, and the elements end up going into the oceans. Have you ever seen reddish-brown rivers? These are full of iron which has been leached – dissolved by water – out of the rocks.

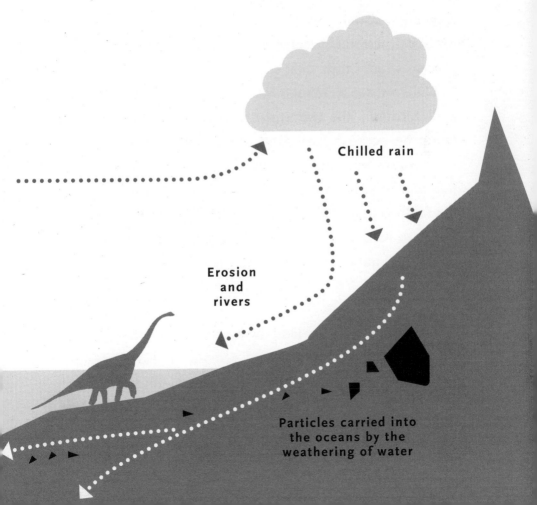

Chilled rain

Erosion
and
rivers

Particles carried into
the oceans by the
weathering of water

Take a sip of fizzy water (those bubbles are carbon dioxide) and see if you can taste the slight sourness. This is acidity; both my sons wrinkle their noses on doing so.

The oceans accumulate all the elements dissolved from the land (and from reaction with the deep ocean floor at hydrothermal vents, such as spectacular black smokers). But only the water molecules themselves keep on moving back to clouds – the elements are left behind. Some elements get so concentrated in the ocean that they turn back into minerals and fall down to the ocean floor as sediments, notably limestone (calcium carbonate) and cherts (silica), a process which limits their concentration in the sea.

Unlike most elements, however, the elements sodium and chlorine – the two ingredients of salt – only fall out from the ocean occasionally and in exceptional circumstances. For example, the entire Mediterranean dried up to a puddle about 6 million years ago after movements in the Earth's crust caused it to be sealed off from the Atlantic Ocean, leaving huge salt deposits. The lack of a continuous natural fall-out of sodium and chlorine means that the sea is always salty.

The weathering of land by water is the very reason why life could appear and remain on Earth: it acts as a thermostat for Earth's temperature. The speed of

Acids and Alkalis

Acids and alkalis are chemical opposites. Adding an alkali to an acid will neutralize the acid, and adding an acid to an alkali will neutralize the alkali.

An acid is a chemical dissolved in water. Many acids can dissolve metals. Mild acids taste sour, but strong acids are dangerous.

An alkali is a compound – a mixture of chemicals. Dissolved in water, strong alkalis can burn or corrode.

weathering depends on Earth's temperature. So if, for any reason, the temperature rises – because, for example, of the increase in the light from the Sun over Earth's history, or if there is an increase of carbon dioxide (a greenhouse gas which warms the Earth) in the planet's atmosphere – then the rocks on land dissolve more quickly. This leads to a rush of elements, including carbon, into the oceans, which in turn speeds up the formation of sediment. This locks additional carbon dioxide into limestone, thus resetting the planet to its previous conditions and stopping everything from overheating.

While weathering maintained temperatures favourable for life to appear, we do not know, and perhaps might never know, where life did begin

Something to Think About

How do you think weathering works to stop the Earth completely freezing over?

on our Earth (there's a challenge for you!). Was it in some 'warm little pond', as the great naturalist Darwin suggested, or in the depths of the ocean? Whichever it was, one thing we do know is that life's origins and evolution depended on water. Elements are bound rigidly in rocks in the Earth's crust, but the ocean is a watery cocktail of all those rocky elements (and organic molecules) highly available, all free to spread out and react. This is the key to initiating life.

Many scientists believe that the deeper oceans are most likely to have provided a safe haven for life's very first stirrings – the surface of the early Earth would have been a much harsher environment. Down in the oceans, harmful radiation was filtered out. The seas also provided buffering against extreme temperatures, and protected the development of life against bombardments of meteorites and intense volcanic outpourings.

From uncertain origins perhaps 2.7 billion years ago, scientists believe that the first 2 billion years of life's history almost certainly played out in the ocean. But inescapable circumstances spurred life to become more and more complex. The increasing success of microbes created more chemical by-products (notably oxygen in the atmosphere), most of which were initially toxic. So, to give more and better control of internal chemistry, simple cells became compartmentalized (these kinds of cells are called eukaryotes) and ended up taking many different forms.

The appearance of multicellular organisms coincided with the most spectacular of life's inventions – that of the skeleton. During this 'Cambrian explosion', 540 million years ago, the rock record of life shows a change from faint ambiguous imprints to a diversity of robust yet intricate shell fossils, undoubtedly sculpted by organisms of complexity (indeed Darwin misread this explosion as the dawn of life).

The Cambrian Era

Scientists divide up the known history of Earth into ages of geological time called eras and periods. The Cambrian period lasted from about 590 million years ago to about 534 million years ago.

The number of Earth's minerals dissolved in water and concentrated in the ocean made making hard parts like shells relatively easy. Just as the horned dinosaurs developed ever-more elaborate ornamentation against the increasing ferocity of the Tyrannosaurs, these first 'biominerals' gave armoured protection against forces, poisons and, importantly, predators.

Skeletons – shells and bones – provided rigidity to support animal life in its first steps on to land!

Over Earth's history, the weathering thermostat has maintained a balance between the amount of acidity (the carbon dioxide) and the amount of alkalinity (the dissolved ions in the ocean). As long as the oceans have been present, they have always been slightly alkaline – perfect for making skeletons.

But we – and future generations on Earth – face a growing problem.

The ever-growing population of the world and our thirst for fossil fuels is adding carbon dioxide – and hence acidity – to the ocean at an unprecedented rate. In a million years or so, the weathering of the land masses of our continents will accelerate sufficiently to start to neutralize this great burp of carbon dioxide into our waters. But this weathering is naturally slow, so in the meantime, the oceans are becoming a bit less alkaline and a bit less saturated. This process is often termed ocean acidification. 'Ocean – slightly less alkalization' would be a more accurate description, though less headline-grabbing!

Think of the continents as an indigestion remedy or 'antacid' for the ocean!

Vulnerable organisms such as coral reefs will find making skeletons increasingly challenging. This could have enormous ramifications across the marine ecosystem. Unless organisms can adapt – and fast!

Some scientists believe we should intervene to redress global warming and acidification by 'geoengineering' carbon dioxide removal. This could include manipulating the weathering of the land to release more alkaline elements into the seas.

But should we really embark on yet another global-scale experiment with our Earth?

What do you think?

. . . and more than a drop to drink!

Just 1 litre of water on Earth contains around 30 million million million million molecules! But a litre of water doesn't look much like a pile of particles – it appears to be a continuous material that can exist as a solid, a liquid or a gas, depending on the temperature and pressure. Add enough heat and water will boil and turn into steam; lower the temperature sufficiently and it will turn into ice.

This is normal behaviour for water; we can observe it easily. But why should all of these 30 million million million million molecules behave the same way? No rebel molecules?

A nineteenth-century Austrian physicist, Ludwig Boltzmann, provided a mathematical explanation of how the enormous number of particles involved actually makes a particular behaviour pattern overwhelmingly the most probable. For although the multitude of particles effectively move entirely at random – each one doing its own thing – it is most likely to produce an average overall behaviour in which individual molecules can be forgotten. In a litre of water, a small fraction of the molecules may randomly and briefly deviate from this average, but the probability that this fraction would be large enough to produce a noticeable change in what we think of as the normal behaviour of water is very, very small.

If the water were to be left alone forever, however, large

random fluctuations would eventually take place – for example, all the molecules could find themselves moving for a short time in the same direction. Now this is a very, very, very low probability, so if you leave a litre of water in a jug, you wouldn't expect to see it suddenly leap out. But if you could leave it for an eternity, such fluctuations would eventually occur – and occur an infinite number of times.

What does this mean for the Universe?

The Universe began 13.8 billion years ago in the Big Bang, and it is expanding at an ever-increasing rate.

If we apply the same principles to our Universe as we just did to water, we can see that a universe that carries on forever would contain every possible random fluctuation, an infinite number of times. This means that a perfect copy of our Universe today – after all, it is a perfectly good arrangement of particles – would eventually appear randomly somewhere else.

A copy of our Universe would obviously include copies of all our human brains, with all their memories too! But as creating all of that randomly is much, much more difficult than forming just one working brain on its own, it would be more probable that these random fluctuations would create single brains, complete with their memories, much more frequently than whole people or copies of the entire Earth.

Ludwig Boltzmann
(1844–1906)

Ludwig Boltzmann was an Austrian physicist and philosopher who was interested in how gases work. Throughout his working life he had a problem – he believed that atoms and molecules existed, and much of his work depended on this. However, there were a large number of scientists at the time who thought atoms and molecules were nonsense. They would not listen when Boltzmann suggested that they think of atoms as models or pictures. Poor Boltzmann spent a great deal of time defending his ideas and proposals from the attacks of these scientists.

Volcanoes on Earth, in Our Solar System and Beyond

Professor TAMSIN A. MATHER

Department of Earth Sciences, University of Oxford

To get volcanoes on any planet, you need a source of heat and something to melt. On Earth the heat is its inner heat (mainly left over from its birth and from ongoing radioactive decay within its rocks). The 'something to melt' is Earth's rocky mantle, the layer of rock under the thin outer crust that we live on. It is mainly solid, but hot enough for it to be able to flow slowly, or creep, a bit like a very sticky liquid. It gets hotter as you go deeper, from a few hundred degrees Celsius (about as hot as or a bit hotter than your oven) to over 4,000°C (7,230°F) (for comparison, the surface of the Sun is about 5,500°C (9,930°F)) just before you reach the outside edge of the molten core. Pressure also increases as you go deeper inside the Earth, like an

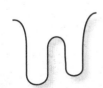

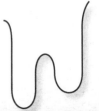

Visiting a Volcano

Imagine what it would be like to visit an erupting volcano. Perhaps you have? The ground shakes with tiny earthquakes as molten lava forces its way from the Earth's insides and hums as volcanic gases struggle to escape. Booming explosions vibrate through your body and ears. Acid fumes sting your eyes and nostrils, and even your skin and sweat begin to smell of sulphur (which smells like rotten eggs and struck matches). Red-hot rocks fly high into the air, turning black as they cool and plummet to the ground. Some of them join the growing cone of rubble. Others feed a lava flow that snakes, clinking and fuming, downhill. This is what it was like for me visiting Mount Etna in Sicily in 2006. It was actually quite a small eruption (otherwise it would not have been safe to get so close!), but breath-taking, even for a volcano scientist (known as a volcanologist)

Earth's Layers

Our planet, Earth, is made up of several layers. At the very centre is the inner core, which might be solid. Around it is the outer core, which may be liquid. Further out is the mantle, which is made of molten rock. Above the mantle is the crust, which is covered by land masses and oceans. The crust is divided into several large sections, called tectonic plates. And all around the crust is the atmosphere.

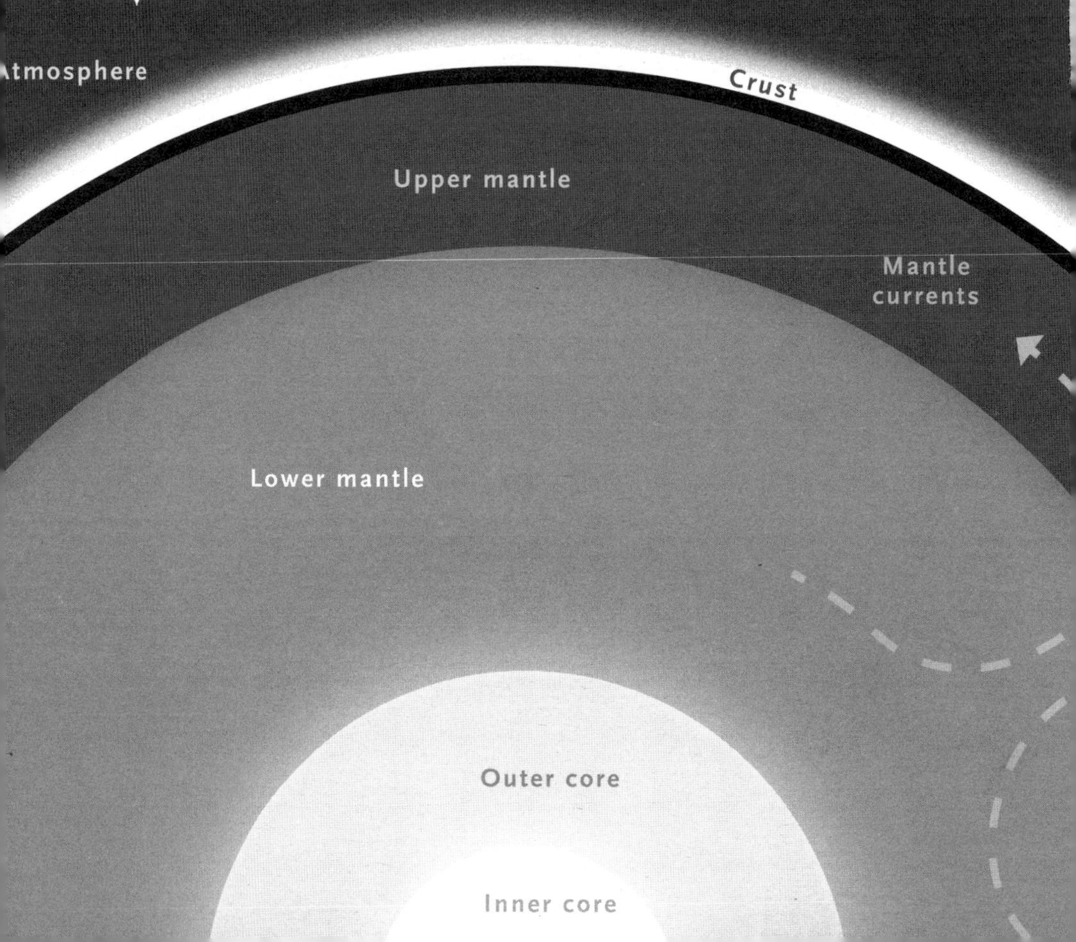

Atmosphere

Crust

Upper mantle

Mantle currents

Lower mantle

Outer core

Inner core

exaggeration of the pressure you feel when you dive to the bottom of a swimming pool.

So the mantle is already very hot, but it is solid. On Earth there are two ways that nature melts it. In some places, like Iceland, where tectonic plates split apart from each other, or beneath Hawaii, where blobs of deep, hot mantle flow slowly upward like a lava lamp, the pressure on the mantle decreases. This makes the mantle's melting point drop.

Did you know that kettles boil at a lower temperature up a mountain as pressure drops?

In other places, like under Japan and Indonesia, things get added to the mantle and make it melt, just as we add salt to roads and pavements in winter to melt ice. This happens at 'subduction zones', where two tectonic plates push together. One sinks below the other and into the mantle, releasing water and other material into the mantle rocks above.

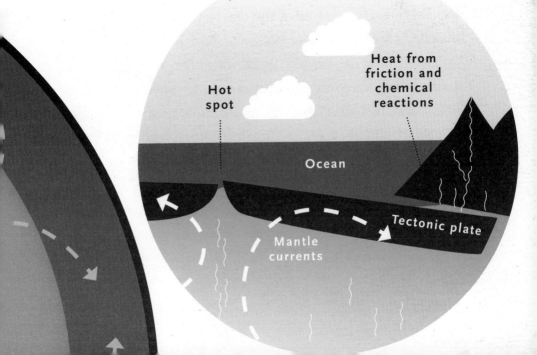

When the mantle melts, it produces a liquid rock called magma. This magma is less dense than the surrounding rock, and so it starts to move up towards the surface. This journey can be relatively quick, especially beneath the oceans where the Earth's crust is thin. Or it can take longer, especially where the crust is thicker, like on the continents. The longer this journey takes, the more time the magma has to cool and change, becoming stickier and stickier.

But what makes magma explode out of the ground rather than just oozing like jam out of a doughnut? Magma has gases like water vapour and carbon dioxide dissolved in it. As magma rises and the pressure drops, the gases can't stay dissolved and they form bubbles. As they rise further, these bubbles grow bigger and bigger until they reach the surface and sometimes explode.

Something similar happens when you open a bottle of cola quickly, especially if someone has been kind enough to shake the bottle first! Sticky magmas are better at trapping gas bubbles. This is one of the reasons why some volcanic eruptions are much more explosive than others.

That's how we explain most volcanism on Earth. But Earth is not the only place in our Solar System that has volcanoes. Just look at a full moon on a clear night. The large dark patches you can see are solidified lava beds. They are called maria, the Latin word for 'sea', because early astronomers thought they really were seas.

On Mars there are huge volcanoes, including Olympus Mons, the largest known volcano.

The Martian Giant

Olympus Mons is about 600 km (370 miles)
wide, and over 22 km (13.6 miles) high – two
and a half times the height of Everest, measured
from sea level – and about the size of Italy, or of
the state of Arizona in the USA.

Olympus Mons

Mount Everest

Being smaller bodies than the Earth, both our Moon and the planet Mars cooled more quickly, so their volcanoes are now dead. Venus is a similar size to Earth, and the results from the Venus Express mission show exciting new evidence of possible active lava flows on this planet.

Further out in the Solar System we see more exotic forms of volcanism on moons orbiting the giant gas planets. The planet Jupiter has volcanoes on several of its more than 60 confirmed moons. Io, the innermost of the planet's larger moons, is the most volcanically active body we know of in the Solar System. Io heats up – like a squash ball in your hand – as it is stretched and squeezed under immense tidal forces from the giant planet it orbits. Io's volcanoes are spectacularly alive, sending plumes of gas and dust hundreds of kilometres into space. Europa, Jupiter's ice-covered moon, is also of great interest. It has a very young surface, with very few craters. This suggests that ice volcanism is continually covering the surface with watery magmas.

In 2005 the Cassini space probe spotted fountains of vapour and ice shooting into space from one of Saturn's moons, Enceladus. And even further away from the Sun, in 1989 the Voyager 2 space probe saw dark plumes rising high above one of Neptune's moons, Triton, maybe made of nitrogen ice and driven by heat from the distant Sun itself.

Recent discoveries of rocky planets outside our Solar System mean that whole new types of volcanism might also exist in the Universe that we and scientists of the future

– like you, perhaps – have yet to discover.
Light that reaches Earth from these planets
can hold clues about their atmospheres. As
volcanoes release distinctive gases, volcanism
could be the first geological process that we
confirm outside our Solar System.

I am often awestruck by how much
remains to be understood about
volcanoes on our own planet. The
idea of a whole universe of
volcanism still out there to
explore is mindboggling!

What Is the Earth Made Of?

Particles, particles, everywhere . . .

very material on Earth is made of tiny objects called atoms. These atoms are constantly knocking each other about by exchanging even smaller particles of electromagnetic radiation called photons, some of which we feel as heat, others we see as light, and others we use for communication by deliberately pulsing them out of radio antennae. Photons and subatomic particles produced by the Sun – and from more distant parts of the Universe – are also constantly flying in from space. So the Earth, other planets, stars and even space are all swirling soups of tiny particles. How can a scientist possibly understand the behaviour of anything when they have to consider such an incredibly large number of microscopic moving parts?

An atom is not an elementary particle because it is made of electrons going round a nucleus in the centre, like the planets go round the Sun. The nucleus is made of protons and neutrons packed tightly together.

Protons and neutrons were previously thought to be elementary particles but we now know they are made of smaller particles, called quarks, held together by gluons, which are the particles of a strong force that acts on quarks but not on electrons or photons.

Elementary particles are the smallest possible things that, as far as we know, cannot be divided up into anything tinier. Examples include the electron, which carries electricity, and the photon, which carries light.

Matter

Matter is made of atoms of various types. The type of atom or element, as it is called, is determined by the number of protons in the nucleus. This can be up to 118, with mostly an equal or greater number of neutrons.

The simplest atom is hydrogen, whose nucleus contains just one proton and no neutron. Scientists think that 90% of the total number of all atoms in the Universe are hydrogen atoms.

The largest naturally occurring atom, uranium, has a nucleus that contains 92 protons and 146 neutrons.

Before stars are born, only the simplest molecules can be found in space. The most common is the hydrogen molecule, which is inside the huge clouds of gas in outer space where stars are born. It consists of two hydrogen atoms joined together.

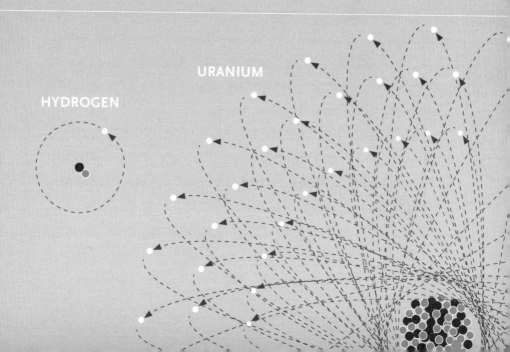

URANIUM

HYDROGEN

Particle Collisions

Scientists study particles and how they behave in machines such as the Large Hadron Collider in Switzerland. The LHC can do things like make particles travel very fast or collide with each other.

If there were no forces, particles colliding inside machines like the LHC would come out the same as they went in. Forces allow fundamental particles to influence each other in collisions (even to change into different particles!) by emitting and absorbing special force-carrying particles called gauge bosons.

Physicists can represent a collision by using Feynman

diagrams. Such diagrams show the ways in which it is possible for particles to scatter off each other. One Feynman diagram is one part of describing such a collision and the diagrams need to be summed up for a complete description of a single collision.

Here is the simplest kind, in which two electrons approach, exchange a single photon, and then continue on their way.

Time goes from left to right, the wiggly line is a photon, and the solid lines show the electrons (marked as 'e'). This diagram includes all the cases where the photon travels up to down or down to up (which is why the wiggly line is drawn vertically):

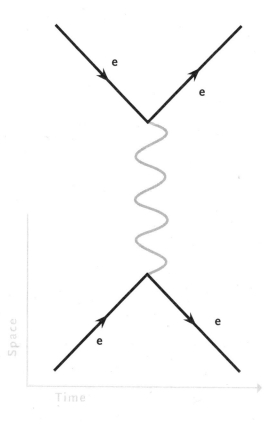

More complicated processes have more than one virtual particle in more complex Feynman diagrams. For example, here is one with two virtual photons and two virtual electrons:

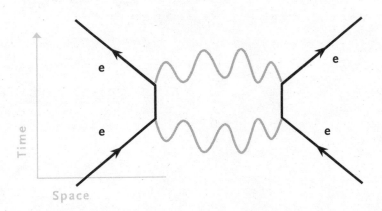

An infinite number of diagrams is needed to fully describe each kind of particle reaction, though thankfully scientists can often obtain very good approximations by only using the simplest ones. Here's one that could represent what might happen at the Large Hadron Collider when protons collide! The letters 'u', 'd' and 'b' are quarks; while 'g' shows gluons.

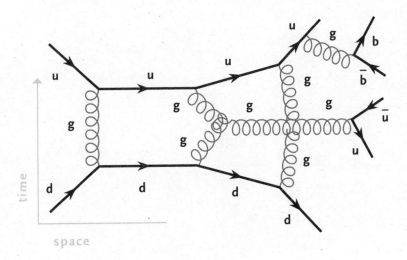

Richard Feynman
(1918—1988)

Richard Feynman was an American physicist who was interested in the way light and matter interact – known as quantum electrodynamics. His work allowed scientists to better understand the nature of particles and waves. As part of his revolutionary work on quantum mechanics, he devised a way of drawing how a particle might move. Feynman diagrams are easy to read and understand. Many of the calculations made about particles and their interactions became much simpler because of Feynman diagrams. He was awarded the Nobel Prize in Physics along with Sin-Itiro Tomonaga and Julian Schwinger in 1965, and became one of the best-known scientists in the world. Richard Feynman also enjoyed playing bongo drums.

The Large Hadron Collider (LHC), CERN

CERN – properly known as the European Organization for Nuclear Research – is an international particle physics laboratory on the border of France and Switzerland, near Geneva.

Founded in 1954, CERN has been operating colliders for well over 50 years as part of its research into fundamental particles.

The initials CERN stand for *Conseil Européen pour la Recherche Nucléai*re. There are 23 member countries.

How We Got to the LHC

In 1983, the Super Proton Synchrotron (SPS) collided protons and antiprotons (the antimatter version of the proton) together and discovered the W and Z particles, which carry the weak nuclear force. The SPS is built inside a circular tunnel 7 km (4.35 miles) in circumference, and today feeds protons to the LHC.

In 1990 a CERN scientist, Tim Berners-Lee, invented the World Wide Web as a way of allowing particle physicists to share information easily – now it's used every day by many people for a plethora of reasons!

After 3 years of digging, a new circular tunnel was completed in 1988. It was 27 km (16.77 miles) in circumference and 100 metres (328 feet) underground. It housed the Large Electron Positron collider (LEP). The LEP collided electrons with positrons (the antimatter version of the electron).

In 1998, work began on digging the detector caverns for the LHC. The LEP was turned off in November 2000 to make way for the new collider in the same tunnel.

The LHC was fully turned on for the first time in September 2008.

The LHC Itself

The LHC is the world's largest particle accelerator.

Two beam pipes run along the circular tunnel of the LHC, each carrying a beam of protons, travelling in opposite directions. It's like a huge electromagnetic racetrack!

Inside the pipes, almost all the air has been pumped out to create a vacuum like there is in outer space, so that the protons can travel without hitting air molecules.

The Large Hadron Collider is the biggest machine in the world.

Because the tunnel is curved, more than 1,200 powerful magnets around the tunnel bend the protons' course so that they don't hit the walls of the pipe. The magnets are superconducting, which means they can generate very large magnetic fields with very little loss of

energy. This requires them to be cooled with liquid helium down to -271.3°C (-456.3°F) – colder than outer space!

At full power, each proton will perform 11,245 laps of the ring per second, travelling at more than 99.99% of the speed of light. There will be up to 600 million head-on collisions between protons per second.

As well as colliding protons, the LHC is also designed to collide lead ions (nuclei of lead atoms).

The core of the LHC is the most lifeless place on Earth!

All in all, there are around 9,300 magnets at the LHC.

The Grid

With about 1 MB of data generated per collision, the LHC detectors produce entirely too much data for even the most modern storage equipment. Computer algorithms select only the most interesting collision events – the rest, more than 99% of the data, are discarded.

Even so, the data from collisions at the LHC in 1 year (2012) reached 15 million gigabytes (which would fill 75,000 PCs, each with a 200GB hard drive). This creates a massive storage and processing problem, especially since the physicists who need the data are based all over the world.

The storage and processing is shared by sending the data rapidly over the internet to computers in other countries. These computers, together with the computers at CERN, form the worldwide LHC Computing Grid.

The Detectors

The LHC has four main detectors situated in underground caverns at different points around the circumference of the tunnel. Special magnets are used to make the two beams collide at each of the four points along the ring where the detector caverns are situated.

ATLAS (A Toroidal LHC ApparatuS) is the biggest particle detector ever built. It is 46 m (51 ft) long, 25 m (80 ft) high, 25 m (80 ft) wide and weighs 7,000 tonnes. It identifies the particles produced in high-energy collisions by tracing their flight through the detector and recording their energy.

CMS (Compact Muon Solenoid) uses a different design to study similar processes to ATLAS (having two different designs of detector helps to confirm any discoveries). It is 21 m (68.9 ft) long, 15 m (49.2 ft) wide and 15 m (49.2 ft) high, but weighs more than ATLAS at 14,000 tonnes.

ALICE (A Large Ion Collider Experiment) is designed specifically to search for quark–gluon plasma produced by colliding lead ions. This plasma is believed to have existed very soon after the Big Bang. ALICE is 26 m (85.3 ft) long, 16 m (52.5 ft) wide, 16 m (52.5 ft) high and weighs about 10,000 tonnes.

LHCb (Large Hadron Collider beauty) – the 'beauty' in the name of this experiment refers to the beauty, or b quark, which it is designed to study. The aim is to clarify the difference between matter and antimatter. It is 21 m (68.9 ft) long, 10 m (32.8 ft) high, 13 m (42.6 ft) wide and weighs 5,600 tonnes.

New Discoveries?

The Standard Model of particle physics describes the fundamental forces (except for gravity), the particles which transmit those forces and three generations of matter particles.

But . . .

Only approximately 5% of the Universe is made from the type of matter we know. What is the rest made of – dark matter and dark energy?

THE UNIVERSE

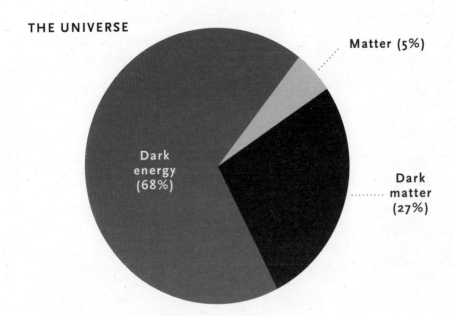

Why do elementary particles have masses? The Higgs boson could explain this. It is a particle predicted by the Standard Model, and its existence was proved in 2012 by ATLAS and CMS.

Why does the Universe contain so much more matter than antimatter? For a very brief time, just after the Big Bang, quarks and gluons were so hot that they couldn't yet combine to form protons and neutrons – the Universe was filled with a strange state of matter called quark–gluon plasma.

The Higgs Boson

In 1964, the British physicist Peter Higgs, who was working on particles at Edinburgh University, predicted that in addition to the particles the scientists already knew about there must be another one. This would give mass to particles, and make sense of all the theories about them. Scientists looked for the new particle, named the 'Higgs boson' for years. In 2012, LHC physicists noticed an interesting signal, which they thought might be the missing particle. It was confirmed as the Higgs boson in 2013.

Quantum Mechanics

Quantum mechanics is the name given to a branch of physics that studies atoms and the particles that make up atoms. It studies the movement of particles and atoms, and the way that atoms take in and give out energy in the form of light. Atoms and particles don't seem to follow the rules that govern bigger things that we can see.

The LHC has recreated this plasma, and the ALICE experiment has been studying it. In this way, scientists hope to learn more about the strong nuclear force and the development of the Universe.

New theories are trying to bring gravity (and space and time) into the same quantum theory that already describes the other forces and subatomic particles. Some of these ideas suggest there may be more than the familiar four dimensions of space–time. Collisions at the LHC could allow us to see these 'extra dimensions', if they exist!

Uncertainty and Schrödinger's Cat

The quantum world is the world of atoms and subatomic particles; the classical world is the world of people and planets. They seem to be very different places!

Classical: we can know both where something is and how fast it's moving . . .

Quantum: we can't know both exactly, and perhaps we know neither – this is Heisenberg's uncertainty principle . . .

C

Classical: a ball travelling from A to B takes a definite path. If there is a wall in the way with two holes, then the ball either goes through one hole or the other . . .

Classical: we know the ball is going to B, and not to somewhere else . . .

Classical: slight observations don't affect the motion of the ball.

Q

Quantum: a particle takes all paths from A to B, including paths through different holes – the paths add up to produce a wave function rippling out from A . . .

Quantum: the particle can reach anywhere the wave function can reach. We only discover where it is when we make an observation . . .

Quantum: observations completely change the wave function – e.g. if we observe our particle at C, the wave function collapses to be completely at C (then ripples out again).

A Cat in a Box!

But cats (classical!) are made of atoms (quantum!). Erwin Schrödinger imagined what this might mean for a cat – though don't do this to your pet cat (Schrödinger didn't actually do it either)! He imagined shutting a cat inside a completely lightproof and soundproof box with some poison, a radiation detector and a small amount of radioactive material. When the detector bleeps (because an atom produces radiation when it decays), then the poison is automatically released. After a while in the box, is the cat still alive? The atoms in the box (including the cat's) take all possible paths: in some, radiation is produced and the poison released; but not in others. Only when we make an observation by opening the box do we discover if the cat has survived. Before that, the cat is neither definitely dead nor definitely alive – in a way, it's a combination of both!

Werner Karl Heisenberg (1901—1976)

Werner Heisenberg was a German scientist who worked in atomic physics. From his work in quantum mechanics, he developed his 'uncertainty principle', which states that the position and momentum of a particle cannot both be determined at the same time. If one has been worked out precisely (or very nearly), the other will be correspondingly less precise, It is therefore better to work on statistical probabilities than to try to work out general laws.

In 1944, Heisenberg gave a lecture in Switzerland, which was neutral in World War II. The Americans sent a special agent with a pistol – and instructions to shoot Heisenberg if it seemed from his lecture that Germany had, or was about to get, an atom bomb. Luckily for Heisenberg, Germany was not even close to creating an atom bomb.

Heisenberg was awarded the Nobel Prize in Physics in 1932.

Erwin Schrödinger
(1887–1961)

Erwin Schrödinger was an Austrian theoretical physicist. He studied quantum mechanics, and he worked out an important equation relating to particles sometimes behaving like waves. Schrödinger did not support Hitler and the Nazis. He escaped Germany before the war, and lived and taught in Ireland, eventually becoming an Irish citizen.

He is most famous for his thought experiment, known as 'Schrödinger's Cat' – scientists are still arguing about what might happen to the cat! In the garden of a house he once lived in in Zurich, there is a life-sized cat – in some lights it is upright and 'alive' and in other lights it is lying down, apparently 'dead'. Schrödinger won the Nobel Prize in Physics in 1933.

M-Theory
– Eleven
Dimensions!

How can we combine Einstein's classical theory of general relativity, which describes gravity and the shape of the whole Universe, with the quantum theory explaining tiny fundamental particles and all the other forces?

The most successful attempts all involve extra space dimensions and supersymmetry.

The extra dimensions are rolled up very tightly so that large objects don't notice them!

String Theory

Today we know of three – or possibly four – dimensions. They are length, breadth, depth and possibly time. Some scientists think that particles aren't like minute dots (which have zero dimensions), but little lines, like tiny pieces of string, which have one dimension. We can't measure them because we haven't yet invented instruments to do so. However, if particles are string-shaped, they could vibrate and interact and it would be possible to have more dimensions in space – maybe up to 11! – than the ones we know.

We can't experience them because they are all bunched up in small spaces.

Supersymmetry would mean more fundamental particles: e.g. photinos to go with photons, and squarks to go with quarks! (The LHC may see these and perhaps even detect extra dimensions.)

The theory of superstrings (supersymmetric strings) replaces particles (dots) with tiny 'strings' (lines). By vibrating in different ways – like different notes on a guitar string – strings behave like different types of particle. Although this sounds strange, strings can explain gravity!

Superstrings must exist in ten dimensions – so six extra space dimensions must be hidden away. We don't understand yet exactly how this happens.

In 1995, Edward Witten suggested that the varied types of superstring theories are all different approximations to a single theory in 11 dimensions, which he called M-theory.

Scientists disagree on what the 'M' means: is it magic, mystery, master, mother or perhaps membrane? Future generations of physicists will discover the truth!

Scientists have studied M-theory very hard since then but still don't know exactly what it is, or if it really is the Theory of Everything that Albert Einstein spent many years trying to work out.

The Building Blocks of Life

Dr TOBY BLENCH
Research Chemist

L ife (plants, animals and humans) is based around the element carbon. Carbon is better at forming very complex and stable molecules than any other element. There is also a lot of it in the Universe – it's the fourth most abundant element. These facts mean that, apart from hydrogen, there are more known molecules containing carbon than all the other elements put together.

However, you need more than just carbon to create life. Another essential is water. Around 60% of the human body is water. It is so important because it is involved in many of the processes that make the body work and also it is involved in, and makes a very good solvent for, the reactions

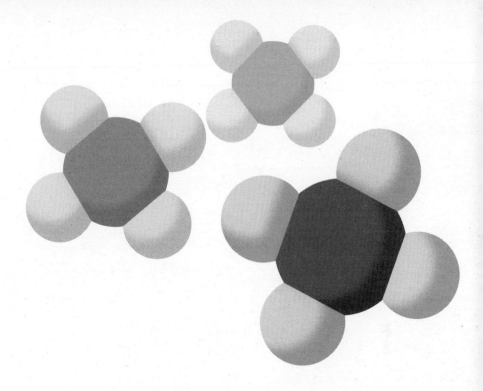

that are needed to make the complex molecules that life is made from.

A very important set of these complex molecules from which life is made are called amino acids, which contain carbon, hydrogen, oxygen, nitrogen and sulphur. There are only 20 different amino acids in the human body but they combine in lots of different ways to make much larger molecules, called proteins. These are found throughout the body and have many different jobs: they help make hair, muscles and ligaments; they help provide structure to the cells in your body; they are in blood; they help you digest your food and they do all sorts of other important jobs in your body.

So this is how, in just a few steps, very simple things like atoms can become something as complex as life.

Temperature

Average temperature on Earth's surface:	15°C (59°F)
Lowest temperature ever recorded on Earth:	-89°C (-128.2°F), Vostok, Antarctica, 21 July 1983
Highest temperature ever recorded on Earth:	70°C (159.3°F), Lut Desert, Iran, 2005
Temperature on the surface of the Moon: daytime average: night-time average:	110°C (230°F) 150°C (-240°F)
Average temperature on the surface of the Sun:	5,500°C (9,932°F)
Average temperature at the core of the Sun:	15,000,000°C (27,000,000°F)
Average temperature of space:	-270.4°C (-454.72°F)

What are chemical elements and where do they come from?

Very simply, a chemical element is a pure substance made from a single type of atom. Why is that interesting? Well, there are only 118 known elements and everything in the world is made from a combination of one or more of these elements. The study of how the known elements behave and make compounds is the science of chemistry.

If everything is made from these elements, where do they come from? The two smallest elements, hydrogen and helium, were formed at the start of the Universe in the Big Bang and some time after they came together in large quantities to form stars. In stars, like the Sun, hydrogen burns at very high temperatures in a process called fusion to make helium. As stars get older, the amount of helium builds up and hydrogen runs out, and so the stars start to use helium as fuel, leading to larger elements like carbon, nitrogen and oxygen. Since these elements are the basis of human life, you could say that we are made of stars!

Depending on how big and hot the star is, larger and larger elements are made in a number of different fusion processes until iron is reached. After that, one of the major ways of forming elements happens when a star explodes. This is called a supernova. A supernova releases the huge amounts of energy that are required to make the heavy elements (elements with atoms that weigh more than an atom of iron).

Atoms are given numbers according to how many protons there are in the nucleus. Atoms of each element have a different number. An atom can also have a weight: it is weighed against a carbon atom. Scientists can use these numbers and weights to make useful lists of atoms.

All these processes account for 94 of the elements, and they all occur naturally on Earth. The other 24, called 'transuranic' as they are heavier than uranium, are man-made with special equipment like nuclear reactors or particle accelerators. These elements are not very stable and fall apart to form smaller, more stable elements in a process called fission. Elements that fall apart in this way are called 'radioactive'. When radioactive compounds fall apart, they also release energy, and that can be used to generate electricity, which is what happens in a nuclear power station.

Why do we weigh different amounts on different worlds?

. **Your weight is the amount of gravitational force between you and the Earth.**

. **Your mass is the amount of matter that you contain.**

Mass is measured in kilos (kg). But isn't weight measured in kilos too? Isn't that confusing? Yes, it is.

Weight is commonly described in kilos on Earth but it really should be given in newtons (N). A newton is a unit of force.

A mass of 1 kg on Earth is about 10 N.

When you travel across the Solar System, your mass doesn't change. But your weight does.

When you land on a planet or moon with weaker gravity than the Earth, your weight changes although your mass stays the same. What does this mean in practice?

If you weigh 34 kg on Earth, here is your weight in kilos on other bodies in our Solar System!

Mercury: 12.8 kg   Jupiter: 80.3 kg

Venus: 30.6 kg   Saturn: 36.1 kg

The Moon: 5.6 kg   Uranus: 30.2 kg

Mars: 12.8 kg   Neptune: 38.2 kg

So you could jump over really high bars with ease on the Moon or Mercury – but find it hard to even take a step over a bar on the ground on Jupiter! (That is, if Jupiter had solid ground – it's made of gas that gets denser as you get closer to the core!)

Flat-Earthers, Moon-Hoaxers and Anti-Vaxxers:

Why Do Some People Reject Scientific Information?

Dr SOPHIE HODGETTS

Lecturer in Psychology, University of Sunderland

Science is an incredible thing, right? By studying biology, chemistry, physics and human behaviour, scientists have made incredible advances in many aspects of life. It is thanks to science that we have been able to destroy certain diseases, travel to the Moon and take incredible images of the Earth. But it might surprise you to learn that there are some people who ask: did we really do all that? There are many people who believe that we have never been to the Moon, and there are many people who believe that the Earth is actually flat! In psychology, the study of the human mind and behaviour, we call this type of belief a conspiracy theory.

A conspiracy theory is an explanation of an event or situation that relies on sinister actors and motivations, rather than hard evidence.

117

There are many different conspiracy theories, but some subjects are more likely to generate conspiracy theories than others. Among the more common topics associated with conspiracy theories are new technologies and scientific achievement. For example, people who believe that we have not been to the Moon argue that NASA staged the whole event, creating fake images and video footage. Similarly, many people who believe the Earth is flat also incriminate NASA, suggesting that evidence showing a flat Earth has been suppressed while evidence showing that the Earth is a globe is actually fake. In many cases, conspiracy theorists state that the reasons for the fakery are money-related; essentially, it's cheaper to fake missions to space than it is actually to do them.

Echo Chambers

In recent years, many scientists have noticed that conspiracy theories are no longer limited to small corners of the internet, but can be found in mainstream news media, on YouTube and social media. This has led some psychologists to believe that the availability of the internet has increased the commonness of conspiracy theories. Although more research is needed in this area, there is some evidence to suggest that social media may have a role to play. For example, if someone joins a Facebook group for people who believe in a specific conspiracy theory, Facebook algorithms will direct that person to more sources of information on that particular topic. Similarly, online groups often become echo chambers for conspiracy theories. An echo chamber is defined as an environment in which someone can only find information that supports their beliefs, as all other information is rejected. In our example, someone in a Facebook group specifically for people who believe in a certain conspiracy theory is likely to become part of an echo chamber for that particular theory.

People have believed in conspiracy theories since before we had the internet, and there are many reasons for this. Psychology studies show that people who are naturally very paranoid or suspicious of others are more likely to believe in at least one conspiracy theory. There is also evidence suggesting that people who are generally very anxious are more likely to believe in a conspiracy theory. This may be because being part of a group of people with similar beliefs can help us to feel less anxious and more supported by the people around us. Conspiracy-theory belief can help someone to feel important, as if they have access to special, unique knowledge that not everybody can have. Because of this, it is also thought that conspiracy-theory belief leads to an 'us versus them' attitude, and this can make a group very strong and more likely to stick together and support each other. Interestingly, there is evidence suggesting that times of social or political unrest are linked to increased belief in conspiracy. It is likely that this is due to the positive effects that being in a group can have on our anxiety levels. It also seems likely that part of the reason that conspiracy theories are more popular these days is the current political unrest and global sense of uncertainty.

Do conspiracy theories matter?

So why does it matter that some people believe in conspiracy theories? Well, let's think about some other examples of science-based conspiracy theories. In a recent survey, one in five Britons stated that they think vaccinations are harmful. Some scientists refer to this as an example of 'science denial', a harmful rejection of science that appears to be increasing in popularity. The evidence that these beliefs are damaging is clear. For example, many parents do not get their children vaccinated to protect them from measles, because they believe the vaccine is dangerous. Recent figures from Public Health England show that between January and October 2018, there have been 913 laboratory-confirmed cases of measles in England alone (compared to 259 such cases in 2017).

Measles

Measles is a very infectious disease. The virus
is carried in the air. Symptoms take 10 days
or a fortnight to appear after you've picked up
the virus, and it takes another 10 or 14 days
before the illness passes. People who suffer
from measles have very high temperatures and
become covered with a red rash. You could also
have a cough, runny nose and inflamed eyes.
You might develop diarrhoea or pneumonia, or
infections of the ears, eyes or brain. These can
leave you with permanent damage to your sight,
hearing or brain. Your ability to resist other infections could be affected. Some people – especially
those who suffer from malnutrition – die from
measles. So far as we know, only humans catch it.
There has never been a case involving animals.

What can we do to help stop the spread of damaging conspiracy theories? This is a difficult question, because many people who believe a conspiracy theory are thinking like scientists! Thinking critically and questioning what we see is a key skill for any researcher, so perhaps 'science denial' is not the right way to think about people who believe a conspiracy theory. Instead, it seems likely that labelling someone in this way will only alienate them. As scientists, we should seek to engage with people who have doubts, or are disappointed by and suspicious of science. It is also very important for scientists to communicate their work effectively, by making it clear how what they do is relevant to other people. Finally, and perhaps most difficult of all, scientists should seek to build trust with their audience. This involves actively speaking out about science, but also resisting any urge to ridicule people who do not share our beliefs as this will not foster trust. Instead, it is important that we listen to them, find out where they got their information from, and consider why they might believe in it. This way, we can start to develop a positive relationship between scientists and the public, and prevent the spread of damaging misinformation.

Part Three

Exploring the Universe

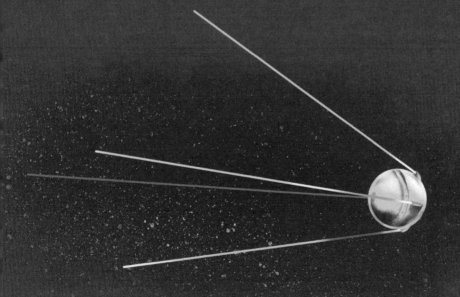

Space Diving

When you go up into space in a spacecraft, you pass through a line which seems to divide the blue of the Earth's atmosphere from the black of space. This is called the Kármán line and it is 100 km (62.1 miles) above the surface of the Earth. It marks the start of space!

Where does space start?

The Earth's atmosphere doesn't just suddenly stop and then you're in space – it's not like putting your head out of a window! No, it gets thinner and thinner the further from Earth you are; but the Kármán line marks the point where 'space' officially begins.

The Kármán Line

Theodore von Kármán (1881–1963), a Hungarian-American engineer and physicist, was interested in aeronautics and astronautics. He tried to work out at what point the atmosphere was too thin to support an aircraft – his answer was 83.6 km (51.9 miles) above Earth. This was changed later to 100 km (62 miles). As well as being important for aircraft and spacecraft, the Kármán line is useful for lawyers – the laws that govern space are not the same as the laws that govern Earth's atmosphere!

To do a space dive or a space jump, you jump out of a spacecraft or hot-air balloon from above the Kármán line, then freefall down through space into the Earth's atmosphere, where you eventually open a parachute to land on the ground.

This is incredibly dangerous! Several space jumps have ended extremely badly indeed.

Is the Kármán line really that high up?

- Yes, Mount Everest, the world's highest mountain, is about 8.85 km (5.5 miles) high. It would need to be almost ten times bigger to reach the Kármán line!

- An average aircraft flies at just under 11 km (6.8 miles) of altitude. So, if you were looking out of the window of a plane, one of these astronauts could have come falling past you!

A space-travel company is now working on a special suit that would allow space diving from even higher altitudes!

But these suits are not for stunts or record breaking – they are being developed as an emergency exit route for astronauts who need to bail out of their space-craft and return to Earth in freefall.

Truly life-saving.

Who has the record for the longest space dive?

- 1960: The record was set by an American, Colonel Joseph Kittinger. Colonel Kittinger was part of a research project into high-altitude bail-outs for pilots. He did three jumps from a helium balloon at over 31 km (19.26 miles) above the Earth! Later, Colonel Kittinger would write that the speed he travelled at was unimaginable.

- 1962: A Soviet colonel called Yevgeni Andreyev set a new record by freefalling further to Earth before opening his parachute than anyone had previously managed. But Joseph Kittinger still kept the record for the longest skydive as Yevgeni Andreyev leaped out of his capsule at 25.48 km (15.83 miles) – not so high up.

- 2012: Joseph Kittinger's record for the longest dive and Yevgeni Andreyev's record for the longest freefall were not broken until this century, when Felix Baumgartner broke them both in one go, jumping from 39 km (24 miles)!

- 2014: He didn't have long as world champion, as a computer scientist called Alan Eustace stole his thunder by completing the highest-altitude jump with the longest freefall only a couple of years later. Eustace fell over 41.419 km (26 miles) in just 15 minutes, his speed peaking at 1,323 km/h (822 mph). People on the ground heard the boom as he went through the sound barrier!

The Night Sky

During the day there is only one star that can be seen in the sky. It is the star that is the closest to us, the star that has the most effect on our daily lives and for which we have a special name: the Sun.

The Moon and the planets do not shine on their own. They appear bright at night because the Sun lights them up.

All the other shining dots in the night sky are stars, like our Sun. Some are bigger, some are smaller, but they are all stars. With the naked eye, on a clear night, away from sources of light like cities, we can see hundreds of them.

In the night sky there are a few objects that can be seen that are not stars – the Moon and the planets, like Venus, Mars, Jupiter or Saturn.

Our Moon

A moon is a natural satellite of a planet.

A satellite is an object that goes round a planet, like the Earth goes round the Sun, and natural means that it is not man-made.

The most obvious effect the Moon's gravity has on the Earth is the tides of the oceans. The sea on the side of the Earth facing the Moon is pulled harder towards the Moon because it is nearer. This raises a bulge in the sea on that side. Similarly, the sea on the side away from the Moon is pulled towards the Moon less because it is further away. This creates another bulge in the sea on the other side of the Earth.

Average distance from the Earth:	384,399 km (238,854 miles)
Diameter at equator:	3,476 km (2,160 miles), which is 27.3% of Earth's diameter
Surface area:	0.074 x Earth's surface area
Volume:	0.020 x Earth's volume
Mass:	0.0123 x Earth's mass
Gravity at equator:	16.54% of Earth's gravity at Earth's equator

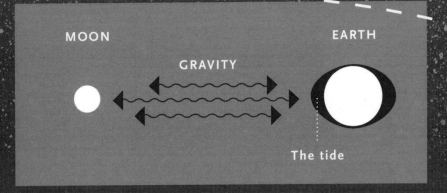

MOON

EARTH

GRAVITY

The tide

Even though the Sun's gravitational pull is much stronger than the Moon's, it has only about half the Moon's effect on the tides because it is so much further away. When the Moon is roughly in line with the Earth and the Sun, the Moon and the Sun tides add together to produce the large tides (called 'spring tides') twice a month.

There is no atmosphere on the Moon, so the sky there is black, even during the day. And there hasn't been an earthquake or volcanic eruption there since around the time life began on Earth. So all living organisms that have ever been on the Earth have seen exactly the same features on the Moon.

From Earth, we always see the same side of the Moon. The first pictures of the Moon's hidden side were taken by a spacecraft in 1959.

The Moon circles the Earth in 27.3 days. The way the Moon shines in the night sky is the same every 29.5 days.

A Moon Quiz

Q: When did our Moon form?

A: It's estimated that the Moon formed over 4 billion years ago.

Q: How did it form?

A: Scientists think that a planet-sized object struck the Earth, causing a dusty hot cloud of rocky fragments to be catapulted into Earth's orbit. As this cloud cooled down, its component bits and pieces stuck together, eventually forming the Moon.

Q: How big is it?

A: The Moon is much smaller than the Earth – you could fit around 49 Moons into the Earth. It also has less gravity. If you weigh 45.36 kg (100 lb) here on Earth, you would weigh around 7.5 kg (less than 17 lb) on the Moon!

Q: Does it have an atmosphere?

A: No. This explains why the sky is always dark on the Moon, meaning that, if you stay in the shade, the stars are visible all the time.

Q: What explanations did people have for the Moon before scientists discovered how it was formed?

A: A long time ago, people on Earth believed that the Moon was a mirror, or perhaps a bowl of fire in the night sky.

For centuries, humans thought the Moon had magical powers to influence life on Earth. In one way, they were right – the Moon does affect the Earth, but not by magic. The Moon's gravity exerts a pull on the oceans, which creates the tides.

Q: Could life exist on the Moon?

A: The Moon cannot support life – unless it's someone wearing a spacesuit. But as a consolation prize, evidence is mounting that the Moon contains much more water – the prime ingredient for life as we know it – than scientists thought just a few years ago. It's frozen, though, and any Earth emigrants to the Moon will need to put substantial effort into transforming it into its life-friendly liquid form.

Q: Has our Moon ever been visited by other civilizations?

A: The Moon has been visited 12 times by astronauts from Earth. Between 1969 and 1972, 12 NASA astronauts walked on the surface of the Moon. Could the Moon have been visited before human civilization even began on Earth, by extraterrestrials who left deposits behind them? Could aliens have got as far as 'next door' to us? It's a very, very long shot, but some scientists on Earth are looking again at moon rock to see whether it holds any clues.

Light and

Light

Everything in our Universe takes time to travel, even light.

In space, light always travels at the maximum speed that is possible: 300,000 km (186,000 miles) per second. This speed is called the speed of light.

It only takes light about 1.3 seconds to travel from Earth to the Moon. Our Sun is further away from us than our Moon is.

When light leaves the Sun, it takes about 8 minutes and 30 seconds to reach us on Earth.

The other stars in the sky are much, much further away from Earth than the Sun. The closest one after the Sun is called Proxima Centauri and it takes 4.22 light years for light from it to reach Earth.

Stars

4.22 light years

Our Sun

All other stars are even further away. The light of almost all the stars we can see in the night sky has been travelling for hundreds, thousands or even tens of thousands of years before reaching our eyes. Even though we see them, some of these stars may not exist any more, but we do not know it yet because the light of the explosion that occurs when a star dies has yet to reach us.

Distances in space can be measured in terms of light years, which is the distance light travels in a year. A light year is around 9,500 billion km (almost 6,000 billion miles).

The Solar System

The Solar System is the cosmic family of our Sun. It comprises all the objects trapped by the Sun's gravity: planets, dwarf planets, moons, comets, asteroids and other small objects yet to be discovered. An object trapped by the Sun's gravity is said to be in orbit round the Sun.

Closest planet to the Sun: Mercury

Mercury is 57.9 million km (36 million miles) away from the Sun on average. Mercury has no moons.

Furthest planet from the Sun: Neptune

Neptune is 4.5 billion km (2.8 billion miles) away from the Sun on average.

Number of planets: 8

From closest to the Sun, the planets are:

Mercury, Venus, Earth, Mars, Jupiter, Saturn, Uranus and Neptune

Distance of the Earth from the Sun:

149.6 million km (93 million miles) on average.

Number of dwarf planets: 6

From closest to the Sun, the dwarf planets are:
Ceres, Pluto, Haumea, Makemake, Eris and Sedna.

Number of known planetary and dwarf planetary moons: 194
Mercury: 0; Venus: 0; Earth: 1; Mars: 2; Jupiter: 79;
Saturn: 82; Uranus: 27; Neptune: 14

Number of known comets: 1,000 (estimated real number: 1,000,000,000,000,000)

Moons of asteroids: 190

Moons of dwarf planets orbiting beyond Neptune: 63

Furthest distance travelled by a man-made object:
more than 21.7 billion km (13.5 billion miles). This is the distance reached by Voyager 1 on 3 June, 2019.
Voyager 1 continued to travel away from the Solar System, transmitting data to Earth.

How our Solar System was created

Step One:

A cloud of gas and dust began to collapse – possibly triggered by shock waves from a nearby supernova.

Step Two:

A ball of dust formed, spinning round and flattening into a disc as it attracted more dust, gradually growing larger and spinning faster.

Step Three:

The central region of this collapsed cloud got hotter and hotter until it started to burn, turning it into a star.

Step Four:

As the star burned, the dust in the disc around it slowly stuck together to form clusters, which became rocks, which eventually formed planets, all still orbiting the star – our Sun – at the centre. These planets ended up forming two main groups: close to the Sun, where it is hot, the rocky planets; and further out, beyond Mars, the gas planets, which consist of a thick atmosphere of gas surrounding a liquid inner region with, very probably, a solid core.

Step Five:

The planets cleaned up their orbits by gobbling up any chunks of material they came across.

Step Six:

Hundreds of millions of years later, the planets settled into stable orbits – the same orbits that they follow today. The bits of stuff left over ended up either in the asteroid belt between Mars and Jupiter, or much further out beyond Pluto in the Kuiper belt.

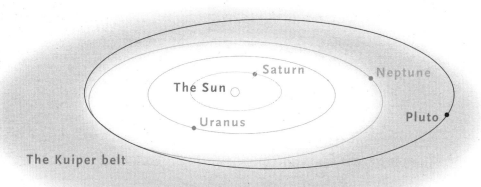

The Kuiper Belt

From the outer edge of Neptune's orbit to about
50 astronomical units (AU) from the outer Solar
System, there is a disc of material left from
when the Solar System formed. It is made up
of scattered icy chunks of frozen gas – some
big enough to form small bodies
that can be classified as dwarf
planets, such as Pluto.

Read more
about AUs on
page 175.

Did you know?

- Our Solar System was formed around 4.6 billion
  years ago.

- Stars with a mass like our Sun take around 10 million
  years to form.

- As Jupiter is the largest planet in the Solar System,
  it may have done most of the cleaning up on its own.

- An exoplanet is a planet in orbit round a star other
  than the Earth's Sun.

Are there other solar systems like ours?

For several hundred years astronomers suspected that other stars in the Universe might have planets in orbit round them. However, the first exoplanet was not confirmed until 1992, orbiting the corpse of a massive star. The first planet around a real, brightly shining star was discovered in 1995, orbiting the star 51 Pegasi. Since then, over 4,000 exoplanets have been discovered – some around stars very similar to our Sun!

This is just the beginning. Even if only 10% of the stars in our Galaxy had planets in orbit round them, that would still mean more than 200 billion solar systems within the Milky Way alone.

Some of these may be similar to our Solar System. Others might look very different. Planets in a binary solar system, for example, might see two suns rise and set in the sky. Knowing the distance from the planets to their star – and the size and age of the star – helps us to calculate how likely it is that we might find life on those planets.

Most of the exoplanets we know about in other solar systems are huge – as big as Jupiter or larger. Large exoplanets are easier to detect than smaller ones. But astronomers are beginning to discover smaller, rocky planets orbiting at the right distance from their star that might be more like Planet Earth.

In early 2011, NASA confirmed their Kepler mission had spotted an Earth-like planet around a star 500 light years away! At only 1.4 times the size of our home planet, this new planet, Kepler-10b, is similar to Earth in size, but it lies very close to its star, and is too hot to sustain any kind of life that we know.

Some of the very big planets that have been discovered may actually be the kinds of small stars known as 'brown dwarfs'.

The Kepler Mission

Kepler was the name given to a space telescope launched by NASA in 2009. It was designed to look for Earth-sized planets orbiting stars in a particular section of the Milky Way. Kepler looked at 530,506 stars and found 2,662 planets. It was in operation for 9 years and was retired when it ran out of fuel in 2018.

Mercury

Vital Statistics

Average distance from the Sun:	57.9 million km (36 million miles)
Diameter at equator:	4,878 km (3,029 miles)
Surface area:	x 0.147 Earth's surface area
Volume:	x 0.156 Earth's volume
Mass:	x 0.055 Earth's mass
Hottest temperature:	430°C (806°F)
Coldest temperature:	-170°C (-274°F)

Mercury is the planet closest to the Sun.
Mercury rotates on its axis very slowly – each 'day' lasts 59 Earth-days.
Mercury orbits the Sun once in 88 Earth-days – a very quick year compared to its slow day!

< Earth (to scale)

Structure

Mercury is the smallest planet. For many years little was known about it, because it orbits so close to the Sun that it was hard for astronomers to see it with telescopes.

Mercury is rocky, and the second-densest planet after Earth in the Solar System. To explain this, scientists think that its core must be iron, and take up 70% of its mass.

Mercury's surface is very similar to that of the Moon, with craters, plains, mountains and valleys. It has the biggest impact crater in the Solar System, the Caloris Basin – which has a diameter of 1,550 km (963 miles). Whatever hit the planet to make the crater produced shock waves so great that on the other side of the planet, opposite the Basin, is an area of very strange hills astronomers call the 'Weird Terrain'.

Between 2011 and 2015 the probe MESSENGER (short for MErcury Surface, Space ENvironment, GEochemistry and Ranging) orbited Mercury. Among its discoveries was the presence of water ice at Mercury's north pole.

Venus

Vital Statistics

Average distance from the Sun:	108.2 million km (67.2 million miles)
Diameter at equator:	12,000 km (7,452 miles)
Surface area:	x 0.902 Earth's surface area
Volume:	x 0.866 Earth's volume
Mass:	x 0.815 Earth's mass
Average surface temperature:	462°C (864°F)

Venus is the second-nearest planet to the Sun.
Venus rotates slowly on its axis – once in 243 Earth-days.
Venus orbits the Sun once in 225 Earth-days. It 'overtakes'
the Earth every 584 days as it orbits.

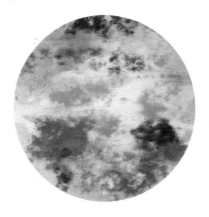

< Earth (to scale)

Structure

Venus is not much smaller than Earth, and as it orbits it comes closest to us of any planet. It is the second-brightest object in the night sky after the Moon. Venus is a rocky planet, surrounded by a very thick, dense atmosphere mostly made of carbon dioxide and drops of sulphuric acid. This reflects light, so it is easy for us to see.

The atmosphere produces a greenhouse effect. The heat on the planet's surface cannot escape, which is why it is the hottest planet in the Solar System. The atmospheric pressure is enormous – over 90 times that of Earth. There is no life and no water on Venus.

Space probes have discovered that much of Venus is covered by volcanic plains. There are two highland areas like continents, one in the northern hemisphere and one just south of the equator.

One unusual feature is that Venus orbits the Sun in a clockwise – or retrograde – direction. Most planets orbit in an anti-clockwise direction.

Venus was the first planet to be visited by a probe (Mariner 2), and the first heavenly body on which a spacecraft landed (Venera 7).

Mars

Vital Statistics

Average distance from the Sun: 227.9 million km (141.6 million miles)

Diameter at equator: 6,805 km (4,228.4 miles)

Surface area: 0.284 x Earth's surface area

Volume: 0.151 x Earth's volume

Mass: 0.107 x Earth's mass

Gravity at equator: 37.6% of Earth's gravity at Earth's equator

Mars is the fourth-closest planet to the Sun.

Mars orbits the Sun once 1.88 Earth-years.

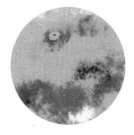

Phobos

< Earth (to scale)

Structure

Mars is a rocky planet with an iron core. In between its core and its red crust there is a thick rocky layer. Mars also has a very thin atmosphere, mostly made of carbon dioxide (95.3%), which we cannot breathe. The average temperature on Mars is very cold: around -60°C (-76°F).

The largest volcanoes in the Solar System are on the surface of Mars. The largest one of all is called Olympus Mons. From one side to the other, it spreads over a disc-shaped area 600 km (370 miles) wide and is 22 km (13.6 miles) high. On Earth, the largest volcano is on Hawaii. It is called Mauna Loa and reaches 4.1 km (2.54 miles) in height from sea level – though if one measures it from where its base starts at the bottom of the ocean, it rises 17 km (10.5 miles) high.

Mars has two small moons: Phobos (named after the Greek god of fear) and Deimos (the Greek god of terror).

Deimos

Conditions on Mars

We know that Mars is now a cold desert planet with no signs of life, simple or complex, on its surface. But was it once a wet, warm world where life flourished? Clues found by man-made Martian rovers, sent out to the red planet to investigate, tell us that Mars was once a very different place.

But could Mars become a fertile, oxygen-rich planet once more, where we could grow crops, breathe the atmosphere and enjoy a balmy Martian summer? Could we 'terraform' Mars so that its atmosphere, its climate and its surface would be suitable for life as we recognize it?

In the case of Mars, we would need to build an atmosphere and increase the temperature of the planet.

Terraforming means making enormous changes to a whole planet in order to create an environment habitable by humans, plants and animals.

To heat up Mars, we would need to add greenhouse gases to the atmosphere to trap energy from the Sun – it's almost the opposite of the problem we have on Earth, where we have too many greenhouses gases in the atmosphere and we want the planet to cool down a little rather than heat up!

But does Mars have enough gravity to retain an atmosphere thick enough for us? Once, it had a magnetic field, but that decayed 4 billion years ago, meaning that Mars was stripped of most of its atmosphere, leaving it with only 1% of the pressure of the Earth's atmosphere. Much lower gravity, then.

In the past, the atmospheric pressure – which means the weight of the air above you in the atmosphere – must have been higher, though, because we can see what appear to be dried-up channels and lakes. Liquid water cannot exist on Mars now as it would just evaporate. To live there, we would need water – and there is lots of water in the form of ice at the planet's two poles. If we went to live on Mars, we could use this. We could also use the minerals and metals that volcanoes have brought to the planet's surface.

So there is enormous potential out there on the red planet, but it's going to be a very difficult job for the first astronauts. Before they can even think about the long-term task of terraforming – if that is even possible – they will have a huge amount of work to do to survive in the red dusty world of our rocky neighbour, Mars. It would be very much like living in some kind of dome with a controlled atmosphere – going out would only be possible with a respirator!

Those astronauts are going to need to be clever, resourceful, brave and persistent in order to build the foundations of a colony or a human habitation on Mars.

Does that sound like you?

Jupiter

Average distance from the Sun: 778.3 million km (483.6 million miles)

Diameter at equator: 142,984 km (88,846 miles), which is 11.2 x greater than Earth's diameter at its equator

Surface area: 120.5 x Earth's surface area

Volume: 1,321.3 x Earth's volume

Mass: 317.8 x Earth's mass

Gravity at equator: 236% of Earth's gravity at Earth's equator

Jupiter is the fifth-closest planet to the Sun.

Jupiter orbits the Sun once in 11.86 Earth-years.

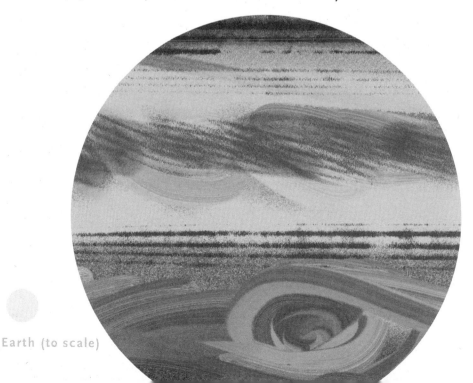

Earth (to scale)

Structure

Jupiter has a small (compared to the overall size of the planet) rocky core surrounded by a liquid metal layer which smoothly turns into a liquid hydrogen layer as height increases. This liquid then turns into an atmosphere made of hydrogen gas that surrounds the planet. Even though it is bigger, Jupiter's overall composition is similar to Saturn's.

The Great Red Spot on Jupiter's surface is a giant hurricane-type storm – a hurricane that has lasted for more than three centuries (it was first observed in 1655), but it may have been there for even longer. The Great Red Spot storm is huge: more than twice the size of the Earth. Winds on Jupiter often reach 1,000 km/h (620 mph).

So far, Jupiter has 79 confirmed moons. Four of them were big enough to be seen by the Italian scientist Galileo in 1610. These are collectively known as the Galilean moons. They are: Io, Europa, Ganymede and Callisto, and they are about the same size as our Moon.

●
< Ganymede   Io   Callisto > ●
●
                              ●
                          Europa

Europa

Is there really life on Europa, the 'blue' moon of Jupiter? Right now, we don't know! Thanks to the Galileo mission, launched in 1989, which sent back lots of new information about Jupiter's fourth-largest moon, we think there is a subsurface ocean under the thick icy crust, which could contain a form of life.

But whether we would actually find fish swimming about if we could land on Europa and drill down through the several-kilometres-thick carpet of ice is anyone's guess! It is far more probable – and, actually, equally exciting to scientists – that any life found would be more like microbes.

But we may get some clearer answers in the next decade! A new mission called JUICE (JUpiter ICy moons Explorer) is planned to set off in 2022 to take a closer look at this mysterious moon. JUICE is a robotic spacecraft designed by the European Space Agency. It will take around 8 years to reach Jupiter, arriving in 2030, and will spend about 3 years looking at the giant gas planet and three of its largest moons, Callisto, Ganymede and Europa. Hopefully JUICE and a simultaneous NASA mission, Europa Clipper, will tell us much, much more about Europa.

What do we know now?

Well, we know that:

- Europa is an icy moon in orbit round Jupiter, the largest planet in our Solar System.

- Jupiter has a total of 79 moons found so far, but the four largest of them – including Europa – are called the Galilean moons, because they were discovered in 1610 by the astronomer Galileo Galilei. When Galileo spotted these moons orbiting Jupiter, he realized that not everything in the Solar System went round the Earth, as previously thought! This completely changed perceptions of our place in the Solar System and the Universe itself.

- Europa is only slightly smaller than our Moon but has a much smoother surface. In fact, Europa may have the fewest lumps and bumps of any object in the Solar System as it doesn't seem to have mountains or craters!

- It has an icy crust. Scientists believe the ocean underneath could be 100 km (62 miles) deep. Compare this to the deepest part of the ocean on Earth, the Marianas Trench in the Pacific Ocean, which is about 11 km (6.8 miles) deep!

- The crust has distinctive markings in the form of dark stripes, which may be ridges formed by eruptions of warm ice at an earlier stage in Europa's life.

Naming Jupiter's Four Big Moons

Although he discovered them, Galileo didn't name Jupiter's four biggest moons. It was another astronomer, Simon Marius, who did that. He also discovered the moons – the day after Galileo did – but didn't publish information about what he had found until 1614.

Saturn

Vital Statistics

Average distance from the Sun: 1,430 million km (888 million miles)

Diameter at equator: 120,536 km (74,898 miles), which is 9.5 x greater than Earth's diameter at its equator

Surface area: 83.7 x Earth's surface area

Volume: 763.59 x Earth's volume

Mass: 95 x Earth's mass

Gravity at equator: 91.4% of Earth's gravity at Earth's equator

Saturn is the sixth-closest planet to the Sun.
Saturn orbits the Sun once in 29.46 Earth-years.

Earth (to scale)

Structure

Saturn has a hot rocky core that is surrounded by a liquid metal layer, which is itself surrounded by a liquid hydrogen and helium layer. Then there is an atmosphere that surrounds the planet.

Winds have been recorded at speeds up to 1,795 km/h (1,116 mph) in Saturn's atmosphere. By comparison, the strongest wind ever recorded on Earth is 400 km/h (253 mph) at Barrow Island off the coast of Western Australia, on 10 April 1996, though it was not officially recognized until 2010. It is believed that wind speeds can sometimes reach 480 km/h (over 300 mph) inside tornadoes. However devastating these winds are, they are still very slow compared to Saturn's winds.

So far, Saturn has 82 confirmed moons. Seven of them are round. Titan, the largest, is the only known moon within the Solar System to have an atmosphere. In volume, Titan is bigger than the planet Mercury and more than three times bigger than our Moon.

Titan

Titan is the largest of Saturn's moons and the second-largest moon in the Solar System. Only Ganymede – one of Jupiter's moons – is bigger.

Titan was discovered on 25 March 1655 by Dutch astronomer Christiaan Huygens. Huygens was inspired by Galileo's discovery of four moons round Jupiter. The discovery that Saturn had moons in orbit round it provided further proof for astronomers in the seventeenth century that not all objects in the Solar System travelled round the Earth, as was previously thought.

It takes 15 days and 22 hours for Titan to orbit Saturn – the same time as it takes for this moon to rotate once on its own axis, which means that a year on Titan is the same length as a day!

Titan is the only moon we know of in the Solar System that has a dense atmosphere. Before astronomers realized this, Titan itself was thought to be much larger in mass. Its atmosphere is mostly made up of nitrogen with a small amount of methane. Scientists think that it may be similar to the atmosphere of the early Earth, and that Titan could have enough material to start the process of life. But this moon is very cold and lacks carbon dioxide, so the chances of life existing there at the moment are slim.

Titan may show us what conditions on Earth were like in the very distant past and help us understand how life began here.

Titan is the most distant place on which a space probe has landed. On 1 July 2004, the Cassini-Huygens spacecraft reached Saturn. It flew by Titan on 26 October 2004 and the Huygens probe detached from the Cassini spacecraft and landed on Titan on 14 January 2005.

Huygens took photographs of Titan's surface and found out that it rains there!

The probe also observed dry riverbeds – 'traces of once-flowing liquid' – on the surface. Cassini imaging later found evidence of hydrocarbons.

In billions of years' time, when our Sun becomes a red giant, Titan might become warm enough for life to begin!

Enceladus

I t's just a tiny white dot orbiting the enormous frozen gas planet Saturn within the densest part of Saturn's rings. It's only one out of Saturn's 82 moons. It's not the biggest or the most visible in the night sky. And yet scientists now think that Enceladus, named after a giant in Greek legend who was buried under the volcano Mount Etna, may be one of the most habitable places in our Solar System! Why? The answer is simple . . .

Water

This snooker ball of a moon – white, round, with an icy smooth surface – seems to have liquid water, one of the most important ingredients for life as we know it. Discovered as long ago as 1789 by the famous astronomer William Herschel, Enceladus remained pretty much a mystery until two Voyager spacecraft passed it in the early 1980s. Voyager 2 revealed that, despite the small size of this little moon, it had all sorts of different landscapes. In some parts, Voyager 2 saw ancient craters; in others, ground that had recently been disturbed by volcanic activity.

Enceladus endures frequent eruptions. But whereas Mount Etna sends hot ashes, lava and gas into the Earth's atmosphere, on Enceladus, cryovolcanoes shoot out plumes of water ice into the atmosphere, some of which float down to the surface as snow. The Cassini space probe, which studied Saturn and the moons and rings around it for 13 years, has taken many photos of the ice fountains of Enceladus. So if you could visit there, you could build a real snowman in space!

A Very Special Place

As well as liquid water, Enceladus may boast all sorts of other useful ingredients for life, such as organic carbon, nitrogen and an energy source, and scientists who study Enceladus recently stated that it makes this moon a very special place. Could it mean there are extraterrestrial life forms on Enceladus? Could there be aliens living deep within this secretive world? Maybe one day you will design a robotic spacecraft which can visit Enceladus and find out if an alien giant is sleeping under the surface of this distant and fascinating little moon!

Planetary Rings

When Galileo looked through his telescope at the sky in 1610, he discovered that Saturn did not look like other planets. For a while, he thought it had ears! Eventually astronomers realized it was surrounded by rings. In the centuries since, we have found out a great deal about them.

They are mostly made from water ice, with a tiny amount of rocky dust, ranging from minute specks up to 10 m (33 ft) chunks. The rings stretch out 6,630 km (4,120 miles) away from Saturn's equator to 120,700 km (75,000 miles), and are on average 20 m (66 ft) thick.

Some of Saturn's moons, like Pandora and Prometheus, orbit within the rings and keep them from spreading out. These moons are called shepherd moons.

There are two theories about the origin of the rings. One is that they may come from a moon of Saturn that was destroyed. The other is that they are material left over from the formation of Saturn.

Saturn is not the only planet to have rings. Jupiter, Uranus and Neptune also have rings, but they are not so numerous and cannot be seen as easily.

Uranus

Vital Statistics

Average distance from the Sun:	2,871 million km (1,782 million miles)
Diameter at equator:	50,800 km (31,547 miles)
Surface area:	x 15.91 Earth's surface area
Volume:	x 63.086 Earth's volume
Mass:	x 14.536 Earth's mass
Average temperature:	-197.2°C (-323°F)

Uranus is the seventh planet from the Sun.

Uranus rotates on its axis once in 17 hours, 14 minutes.

Uranus orbits the Sun once in 84 Earth-years.

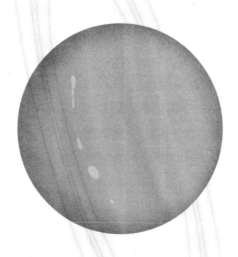

Earth (to scale)

Structure

Uranus was known to astronomers in the ancient world, but they thought it was a star. It may have been recorded in 128 BCE by the Greek Hipparchus in his star catalogue – this was taken over and expanded by Ptolemy in the second century AD. Sir William Herschel recorded and described it in 1781, but at first he thought it was a comet!

Uranus has the coldest atmosphere of any planet in the Solar System, and very high winds have been recorded: 900 km/h (560 mph).

The spacecraft Voyager 2 flew by Uranus in 1986: photographs show a bluey-green planet with no markings at all. Scientists think there might be a small rocky core at the centre. This is surrounded by a thick layer of frozen water, ammonia and methane. The outer layer of the atmosphere is mostly hydrogen and helium.

Uranus is one of the two planets called 'ice giants', and its axis is tilted at such an angle that the planet seems to be lying on its side. Like Venus, Uranus orbits the Sun in a clockwise, or retrograde, direction.

Uranus has 27 known moons, and at least 13 dark rings, which cannot be seen from Earth.

Neptune

Vital Statistics

Average distance from the Sun:	4,486 million km (2,786 million miles)
Diameter at equator:	48,600 km (30,199 miles)
Surface area:	x 14.98 Earth's surface area
Volume:	x 57.74 Earth's volume
Mass:	x 17.147 Earth's mass
Average temperature:	-201°C (394°F)

Neptune is the eighth planet from the Sun.

Neptune rotates on its axis once every 18 to 20 hours.

Neptune orbits the Sun once in 164.8 Earth-years.

Earth (to scale)

Structure

In many ways, Neptune is very like Uranus. It is also an ice giant, and scientists think it too has a small rocky core, surrounded by frozen water, ammonia and methane, with an atmosphere mostly of hydrogen and a little helium. Tiny amounts of methane in the atmosphere make the planet look blue.

Voyager 2 flew by Neptune in 1989, and information from this, as well as more recent information from the Hubble Space Telescope and powerful telescopes on Earth, have shown weather patterns, including the Great Dark Spot, an enormous storm system, the Small Dark Spot (another storm), and the Scooter, a storm marked by a group of white clouds moving very fast.

Winds on Neptune have been measured at almost supersonic speeds: 2,200 km/h (1,300 mph). Mostly the winds blow in a retrograde direction, against the planet's rotation.

Neptune has 14 known moons, and four very faint rings.

One of Neptune's moons, Triton, is the only moon in the Solar System to have a clockwise (retrograde) orbit.

Pluto

Our Moon

Earth (to scale)

Before August 2006 there were said to be nine planets that revolved round the Sun: Mercury, Venus, Earth, Mars, Jupiter, Saturn, Uranus, Neptune and Pluto. These nine celestial bodies still exist, of course, and are exactly the same as they were before, but in August 2006 the International Astronomical Union decided not to call Pluto a planet any more. It is now called a dwarf planet.

This is because of a change in the definition of what a planet is. There are now three rules that need to be fulfilled by any object in space in our Solar System in order to be called a planet:

1) It has to be in orbit round the Sun.

2) It has to be big enough for gravity to make it almost round and stay that way.

3) Its gravity has to have attracted almost everything that is next to it in space as it travels round the Sun, so that its path is cleared.

According to this new definition, Pluto is not a planet. Is it in orbit round the Sun? Yes. Is it almost round and will it stay so? Yes. Has it cleared its path round the Sun? No: there are many rocks around in its orbital path. So because it failed the third rule, Pluto has been downgraded from a planet to a dwarf planet.

The other eight planets fulfil the three rules and so they remain planets. For planets and stars other than the Sun, an additional requirement has been agreed upon by the International Astronomical Union: the object should not be so big as to become a star itself at a later stage.

Bits and Pieces

As well as the planets and their moons, there are other objects orbiting the Sun. Asteroids are bodies ranging in size from dust particles to dwarf planets. One very large group of asteroids formed of rock and metal is the asteroid belt, which lies between Mars and Jupiter. Here, there could be nearly 2 million asteroids bigger than 1 km (0.6 miles) in diameter. Some of the asteroids are large enough to have names, and one, Ceres, is classed as a dwarf planet. It is nearly 1,000 km (600 miles) across. Scientists think asteroids are remnants left over from the formation of planets in the Solar System.

Far out in the Solar System, beyond Neptune, lies the Kuiper belt. This is very much bigger than the asteroid belt – at least 20 times as wide, and possibly 200 times more massive! The small objects found here are mostly made of ice – frozen water, ammonia and methane. They are also considered to be left over from the formation of the Solar System. The dwarf planet Pluto lies in the Kuiper belt.

Exoplanets

Planets around stars other than our Sun are called exoplanets. As of 2019, 4,071 exoplanets have been seen. Most of them are huge – much bigger than the Earth.

CoRoT

In December 2006 a satellite named CoRoT (short for Convection, Rotation and planetary Transits) was sent into space. It was a space telescope. The mission lasted until 2013, when CoRoT had to be retired because a computer failed and no information could be received from its telescope. CoRoT made many discoveries, including 32 exoplanets that could be confirmed by using ground-based telescopes. Several hundred more possibilities are being investigated. CoRoT 7b, discovered in 2009, was the first exoplanet that could be proved to be made of metal or rock.

Alpha Centauri

Alpha Centauri A

Alpha Centauri B

At just over 4 light years away, Alpha Centauri is the closest star system to our Sun. In the night sky it looks like just one star, but is in fact triplets. Two Sun-like stars, Alpha Centauri A and Alpha Centauri B – separated by around 23 times the distance between the Earth and the Sun – orbit a common centre about once every 80 years. There is a third, fainter, star in the system, Proxima Centauri, which orbits the other two but at a huge distance from them. Proxima Centauri is the nearest of the three to Earth.

Alpha B is an orange star, slightly cooler than our Sun and a bit less massive. It is thought that the Alpha Centauri system formed around 1,000 million years before our Solar System. Both Alpha A and Alpha B are stable stars, like our Sun, and like our Sun may have been born surrounded by dusty, planet-forming discs.

In 2008 scientists suggested that planets may have formed around one or both of these stars. From a telescope in Chile, they are now monitoring Alpha Centauri very carefully to see whether small wobbles in starlight will show us planets in orbit in our nearest star system. Astronomers are looking at Alpha Centauri B to see whether this bright, calm star will reveal Earth-like worlds around it.

Alpha Centauri can be seen from Earth's southern hemisphere, where it is one of the stars of the Centaurus constellation. Its proper name – Rigel Kentaurus – means 'centaur's foot'. Alpha Centauri is its Bayer designation (a system of star-naming introduced by astronomer Johann Bayer in 1603).

Alpha A is a yellow star and very similar to our Sun but brighter and slightly more massive.

Alpha A and Alpha B are binary stars. This means that if you were standing on a planet orbiting one of them, at certain times you would see two suns in the sky!

Proxima Centauri is a small star – a red dwarf. Scientists think it takes about a million years to orbit the other two Centauri stars.

So far the only planet found in the Alpha Centauri system is one that orbits Proxima Centauri. It is a little bit bigger than Earth, and lies in the habitable zone, where water might exist.

Proxima
Centauri

55 Cancri

55 Cancri is a star system 41 light years away from us in the direction of the Cancer constellation. It is a binary system: 55 Cancri A is a yellow star; 55 Cancri B is a smaller, red dwarf star. These two stars orbit each other at 1,000 times the distance between the Earth and the Sun.

This star system is a good example of one that has been found to have a family of planets. On 6 November 2007, astronomers discovered what was then a record-breaking fifth planet in orbit round the star Cancri A.

The first planet around Cancri A was discovered in 1996. Named Cancri b, it is the size of Jupiter and orbits close to the star. In 2002, two more planets (Cancri c and Cancri d) were discovered; in 2004, a fourth planet was found, Cancri e, which is the size of Neptune and takes just three days to orbit Cancri A. This planet would be scorchingly hot, with surface temperatures up to 1,500°C (2,732°F).

The fifth planet, Cancri f, is around half the mass of Saturn and lies in the habitable – or Goldilocks – zone of its star. This planet is a giant ball of gas, mostly made of helium and hydrogen, like Saturn in our Solar System. But there may be moons in orbit round Cancri f or rocky planets within Cancri's Goldilocks Zone, where liquid water could exist on the surface.

Learn more about the Goldilocks zone on page 66.

Cancri f orbits its star at a distance of 0.781 astronomical units (AU). An astronomical unit is the measure of distance that astronomers use to talk about orbits and distance from stars.

Given that there is life on Earth and liquid water on the surface of our planet, we can say that 1 AU or 150 million km (93 million miles) from our Sun is within the habitable zone of our Solar System. So, for stars of roughly the mass, age and luminosity of our Sun, we can guess that a planet orbiting its star at around 1 AU might be in the Goldilocks Zone. Cancri A is an older and dimmer star than our Sun, and astronomers calculate that its habitable zone lies between 0.5 AU and 2 AUs away from it, which puts Cancri f in a good position!

It is very difficult to spot multiple planets around a star because each planet produces its own stellar wobble. To find more than one planet, astronomers need to be able to spot wobbles within wobbles! Astronomers in California have been monitoring 55 Cancri for over 20 years to make these discoveries.

1 AU = the average distance from the Earth to the Sun

Kepler-90

More exoplanets are regularly discovered. The record for the most exoplanets is currently held by Kepler-90, a star in the constellation Draco. It has eight planets, the same number as our Sun. The eighth planet was discovered in 2017. Which star will break the record next?

Andromeda

The Andromeda Galaxy (also known as M31) is the nearest large galaxy to our own Milky Way, and together they are the largest objects in our Local Group of galaxies. The Local Group is a number – at least 40 – of nearby galaxies which are strongly influenced by each other's gravity.

The Messier Catalogue

The French astronomer Charles Messier (1730–1817) was interested in comets. He kept finding objects in the sky that weren't comets – they got in his way as he hunted – so he made a list of them. Now we know they were such things as galaxies, nebulae and star clusters. Messier's list of 110 objects – with 'M' for Messier in front of them, is a handy way to refer to them, and scientists have added many more to the original list.

At 2.5 million light years away, Andromeda is not actually the closest galaxy to us (that title probably goes to the Canis Major Dwarf Galaxy), but is the closest with a comparable size and mass.

Current estimates suggest that the Milky Way has more mass (including dark matter), but Andromeda has more stars.

Andromeda has a spiral shape, like the Milky Way.

Like the Milky Way, Andromeda has a supermassive black hole at its centre.

Also like the Milky Way, Andromeda has several (at least 14) satellite dwarf galaxies in orbit round it.

Unlike most galaxies, light received from Andromeda is blue-shifted. This is because the expansion of the Universe – which makes galaxies move away from each other – is being overcome by gravity between the two galaxies, and Andromeda is falling towards the Milky Way at around 300 km (186 miles) per second. The two galaxies may collide in around 4.5 billion years, and eventually merge – or they may just miss. Collisions between galaxies are not thought to be unusual – the small Canis Major Dwarf Galaxy appears to be merging with the Milky Way right now!

Satellites in Space

A satellite is an object that orbits (or revolves) round another object, like the Moon round the Earth. The Earth is a satellite of the Sun. However, we tend to use the word 'satellite' to mean the man-made objects that are sent into space on a rocket to perform certain tasks, such as navigation, weather monitoring or communication.

Rockets were invented by the ancient Chinese in around 1000 AD. Many hundreds of years later, on 4 October 1957, the Space Age began when the Russians used a rocket to launch the first satellite into orbit round the Earth. Sputnik, a small sphere capable of sending a weak radio signal back to Earth, became a sensation.

At the time, it was known as the 'Red Moon' and people all over the world tuned their radios to pick up its signal. The Mark I telescope at Jodrell Bank in the UK was the first large radio telescope to be used as a tracking antenna to chart the course of the satellite. Sputnik was quickly followed by Sputnik II – also called 'Pupnik' because it had a passenger on board! Laika, a Russian dog, became the first living being from Earth to travel into space.

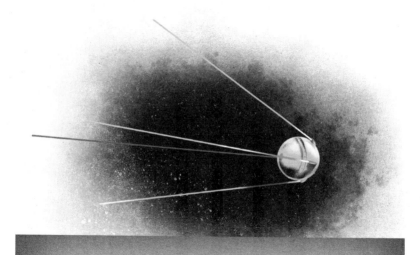

Did you know?

The first person to publish a study of the mathematics for an artificial satellite was Sir Isaac Newton. 'Newton's Cannonball' was described in his book *A Treatise of the System of the World*, published in 1687. His idea is a thought experiment.

The Americans tried to launch their own satellite on 6 December 1957 but the satellite only managed to get 1.2 m (3.9 ft) off the ground before the rocket exploded. On 1 February 1958, Explorer I was more successful, and soon the two superpowers on Earth – the USSR and the USA – were also competing to be the greatest in space. At that time, they were very suspicious of each other and soon realized that satellites were good for spying. Using photographs taken from above the Earth, the two superpowers hoped to learn more about activities in the other country. The satellite revolution had begun.

Satellite technology was originally developed for military and intelligence reasons. In the 1970s the US government launched 24 satellites, which sent back time signals and orbital information. This led to the first global positioning system (GPS). This technology, which allows armies to cross deserts by night and long-range missiles to hit targets accurately, is now used by millions of ordinary people to avoid getting lost! Known as satellite navigation – or satnav – it also helps ambulances to reach the injured more promptly and coastguards to launch effective search-and-rescue missions.

Other Uses for Satellites

Communication across the world was also changed forever by satellites. In 1962 a US telephone company launched Telstar, a satellite that broadcast the first-ever live television show from the US to Britain and France. The British saw only a few minutes of fuzzy pictures but the French received clear pictures and sound. They even managed to send back their own transmission of Yves Montand singing 'Sous le ciel de Paris' ('Relax, You Are in Paris')! Before satellites, events had to be filmed and the film taken by plane to be shown on television in other countries. After Telstar, major world events – such as the funeral of US President John F. Kennedy in 1963, or the football World Cup in 1966 – could be broadcast live across the globe for the first time. Mobile phones and the internet are other ways in which you might be using a satellite today.

Satellite imaging isn't only used by spies! Being able to look back at the Earth from space has enabled us to see patterns, both on the Earth and in the atmosphere. We can measure land use and see how cities are expanding and how deserts and forests are changing shape. Farmers use satellite pictures to monitor their crops and decide which fields need fertilizer.

And satellites have transformed our understanding of the weather. They have made weather forecasts more accurate and shown the way weather patterns emerge and move around the world. Satellites cannot change the weather but they can track hurricanes, tornadoes and cyclones,

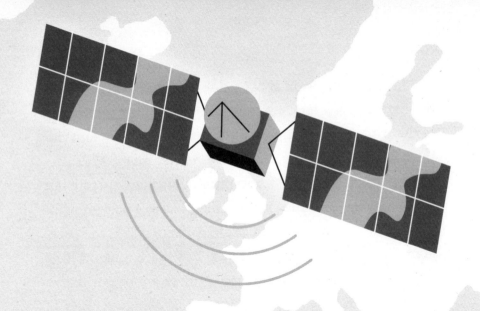

giving us the ability to issue severe-weather warnings.

In the late 1990s NASA's TOPEX/Poseidon satellite, which maps the oceans, provided enough information for weather watchers to spot the El Niño phenomenon. And a new series of NASA satellites, all named Jason, have been launched in this century to gather data about the ocean's role in determining the Earth's climate. This in turn will help us to better understand climate change, showing us detailed images of the melting polar ice caps, disappearing inland seas and rising ocean levels – information we now need urgently!

Just as satellites can look back at the Earth and transform our understanding of our own planet, so they have also changed our perception of the Universe around us. The Hubble Space Telescope was the first large-scale space observatory. Orbiting the Earth, Hubble has helped astronomers to calculate the age of the Universe and has shown that it is expanding at an accelerated pace.

There are at present about 5,000 satellites in orbit round the Earth, with a total coverage of every square centimetre of the planet. It is getting quite crowded out there and can be dangerous. Satellites in low Earth orbit move very fast – around 29,000 km/h (18,000 mph). Collisions are rare but when they happen, they make a mess! Even a fleck of paint moving at that speed could cause damage if it hit a space-craft. There may be a million pieces of space junk orbiting the Earth, but only about 9,000 of these are bigger than a tennis ball. Now, there are scientists working on ways of collecting space junk and getting rid of it.

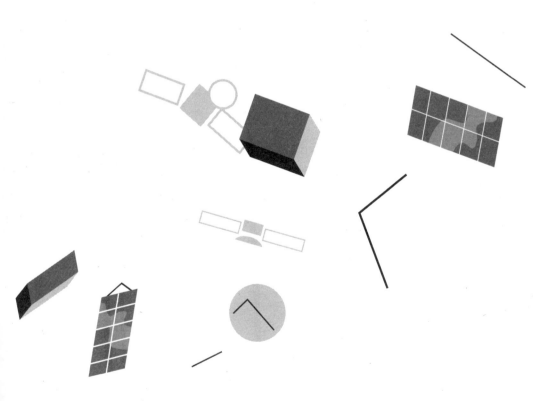

The Multiverse

Professor THOMAS HERTOG

Theoretical Physics, KU Leuven University

s it possible that our Universe is part of a vastly larger physical reality, made up of countless other universes lying far beyond the one we know? The idea of a multiverse profoundly challenges our understanding. After all, we usually think of our Universe as all there is. Everything.

But today's leading scientific cosmological theories predict the existence of a multiverse. Like our planet, star, and Galaxy, our Universe may be just one of many. At the same time, the multiverse idea remains deeply controversial among scientists. This is because the idea of a multiverse seems to limit what science has to say about our world.

In short, understanding the basic nature of the multiverse and our place within this enigmatic whole is one of the great science questions of our time.

Some scientists even argue that the idea of a multiverse should not be regarded as science at all, since we can't hop from one universe to another.

How the Idea Started

The idea that we may be living in a multiverse emerges from the revolutionary insights in cosmology in the twentieth century, starting with the discovery in the 1920s that our Universe is expanding. The expansion means more space is created as time goes on, causing galaxies to recede from each other. But cosmic expansion also implies that the Universe must have been in a radically different state in the distant past. Tracing its evolution backwards in time, Einstein's theory of general relativity predicts that our expanding Universe must have had a beginning, about 13.8 billion years ago, when the exceedingly high densities of matter destroyed the basic fabric of space and time. This cosmic origin became known as the Big Bang.

The finite speed of light, and the finite age of the Universe, mean that astronomers can peer at stars and galaxies only within a limited distance. This distance is our cosmic horizon, which takes us as far as we can go in our observable Universe. Were space static, the cosmic horizon would be 13.8 billion light years away, but because of the expansion of space it is 42 billion light years away.

Read more about the Big Bang on page 23.

Quantum Theory Again

At the Universe's origin, the macroscopic world of stars and galaxies merges with the microscopic world of atoms and particles. Whereas Einstein's theories of relativity governs the former, the behaviour of particles is described by quantum theory. At the Big Bang, the entire Universe must have been something like a giant particle. Therefore to describe the extreme conditions at the Big Bang, we ought to combine the Einsteinian view of the world with quantum theory to make a single overarching framework that is both quantum and gravity.

But quantum theory predicts probabilities for different outcomes. In the quantum theory of particles, these could be the probabilities of finding an electron in one place or another. Applied to the Universe as a whole, however, the outcome is an entire separate universe! From the quantum fuzz at the beginning, widely different universes can evolve. Quantum theory predicts not a single Big Bang but many Big Bangs, giving birth to a variety of different universes, each with its own history. The multiverse emerges as an almost inescapable consequence of our Universe's quantum origin.

Where – and what – are they?

Where are the universes making up the multiverse? Some scientists argue the other universes are simply very far away. These are models of the cosmos in which space stretches well beyond our cosmic horizon and perhaps even to infinity. If that were true, there might be an infinite number of Earths with readers reading this book on them. These other Earths would be like isolated universes, lying beyond each other's cosmic horizon. Others argue that different universes are hovering only millimetres away from us, but in some extra dimension where light cannot penetrate. String theory – today's most promising quantum gravity theory – predicts the existence of such extra dimensions, providing ample space for universes to hide.

Alternatively, any notion of location of other members of the multiverse relative to us may have no meaning. This is the most radical vision of the multiverse and it is the one most fundamentally implied by quantum theory. In this vision, the multiverse is like a branching tree, in which each branch corresponds to a different universe representing an entire cosmic evolution. 'There are many histories, and the universe lives them all,' Stephen Hawking once said.

There's more about string theory on page 108 in Part Two.

What kind of universes can come into existence? Are

the laws of physics the same across the entire multiverse tree? Probably not. The laws of physics are a concise set of rules describing gravity and the elementary particles, and how they interact. In string theory, these laws are specified by the shape of the extra curled-up dimensions. Since string theory allows for a vast range of different shapes of the extra dimensions, it naturally predicts a multitude of widely different universes. String theorists are currently investigating what physical features can vary from one universe branch to another in the multiverse. The laws of physics in each of the universes are forged in the heat of their Big Bang. The matter around us as well as the overall architecture of our Universe are to some extent the accidental outcomes of how our particular Universe came into existence.

Why should we care at all about the multiverse if we can't see universes other than our own? Why can't we simply cut out a single universe – ours – and forget about all other universes? The quantum theory behind the multiverse does not allow us to prune the multiverse tree! The physically distinct universes that make up the multiverse are mathematically united in a single overarching framework that tells us how widespread one kind of universe is, relative to another. This gives us the grip on the multiverse that will be crucial to turn the idea into a scientific model that could be proved.

Our Own Improbable Universe

I hasten to add that we may not live in the most probable of all universes! We must find ourselves in a realm of the multiverse where the laws of physics favour the emergence of complexity and life. This requires a delicate balance between the various particle forces and gravity, selecting the habitable branches of the multiverse. We evolved together with the multiverse, and I predict that when the multiverse idea is eventually put on solid scientific ground, it will reveal a profound connection between our existence as observers within one of its universes and the laws of physics which led to our being here.

Do you know another universe?

It's not just scientists who theorize about multiverses. Many story tellers write about them, often calling them 'parallel universes' or 'parallel worlds'. Have you ever come across a parallel world in a book or a comic? What things are the same as our world and Universe – and what things are different?

Part Four

Dark Matters

The Dark Side of the Moon

It sounds like it should always be night on the dark side of the Moon, but that's not true, as any friendly astronomer will tell you. First of all, astronomers don't talk about the dark side. They call it the far side of the Moon, because the far side of the Moon has night and day, just like we do on Earth.

When we look up at the Moon in the night sky, it looks familiar to us, no matter where we are on the Earth. We see the same features each time because we are always looking at the same side of the Moon. So how come we never get to see the other side of our old friend the Moon?

Why can't we see the far side?

The Moon orbits the Earth while rotating on its axis. It takes the Moon the same amount of time to complete one orbit of the Earth as it does for our rocky satellite to rotate – about 29 days. If the Moon didn't rotate, we would see all of its faces or sides, near and far, as the Earth rotates while orbiting the Sun. But because the Earth is turning and the Moon is turning – and the gravity of the Earth has slowed down the Moon's rotation to its current speed – it means we always see the same face of the Moon.

Phases of the Moon

The positions of the Earth as it orbits the Sun and the Moon as it orbits the Earth give us the phases of the Moon.

- When the Moon is between the Earth and the Sun, we call it a new moon. The Moon looks dark to us from Earth as it is lunar night-time on the near side of the Moon (the side nearest to us).

- When the Earth is between the Sun and the Moon, that's a full moon. If you were standing on the near side of the Moon, we might be able to see you from Earth as you would be standing in the midday sunshine of a lunar day!

Even though we can't see the far side of the Moon, it has been visited by astronauts. One of them said it reminded him of his kids' sandpit!

Full
moon

As
seen from
Earth

Midnight

Midday

Sunrays

Sunrays

As
seen from
Earth

New
moon

The Sun

The Dark Side of the Universe

Dr PAUL DAVIES

Department of Physics, Arizona State University, USA

We've already looked at atoms, but let's see how they work in more detail ...

What is the world made of?

One of the simplest questions we can ask is: what is the world made of?

Long ago, the Greek Democritus hypothesized that everything is made of indivisible building blocks he called atoms. He was right – and over the past 2,000 years we have filled in the details.

All the stuff in our everyday world is made of

combinations of the 94 different types of atoms: the elements of the periodic table – hydrogen, helium, lithium, beryllium, boron, carbon, nitrogen, oxygen and all the way up to uranium, number 94. Plants, animals, rocks, minerals, the air we breathe and everything on Earth is made of these 94 building blocks. We also know that our Sun, the other planets in our Solar System and other stars far away are made of the same 94 chemical elements. We understand atoms very well, and we are masters at rearranging them into all kinds of different things. The science of chemistry is all about building different things with atoms, a kind of 'Lego with atoms'.

The Periodic Table

The periodic table is a list of all the elements in order of the weight of their atoms. Hydrogen is the lightest element, and plutonium is the heaviest. As well as the 94 elements that occur naturally, scientists have created another 24 in laboratories.

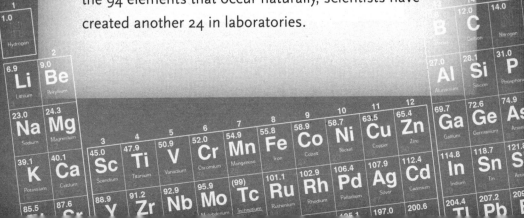

Dmitri Mendeleev
(1834–1907)

Dmitri Mendeleev was a Russian chemist. He was born in Siberia, the youngest of about 17 children, but his family had to move right across Russia to St Petersburg when his father, a schoolteacher, went blind.

He studied chemistry in Russia and Germany, eventually becoming a professor at St Petersburg University, where he taught inorganic chemistry. By 1870, the university was internationally recognized for chemical research.

In 1867, Mendeleev started writing a chemistry textbook. While he was working on the 65 known chemical elements, he wrote each one, with its properties, on a card. Moving the cards around, he noticed that they seemed to form patterns. After working on the cards for hours, he fell asleep at his desk, but his mind went on working. 'I saw in a dream a table where all elements fell into place as required. Awakening, I immediately wrote it down on a piece of paper, only in one place did a correction later seem necessary.' When he woke up, he arranged the cards in a table according to their atomic weights.

Studying his table, Mendeleev was able to predict the existence of eight elements that hadn't been discovered. He presented his work, which he called the periodic system, to the Russian Chemical Society in 1869. What we now call the periodic table had arrived.

Mendeleev was interested in many aspects of life in Russia. He introduced the metric system and also helped found the first oil refinery in the country, though he is said to have commented that burning petroleum as a fuel 'would be akin to firing up a kitchen stove with bank notes'.

He received many honours for his work, but not the Nobel Prize – when he was proposed for the prize, one person with whom he'd disagreed argued so fiercely against him that the prize was awarded to another scientist. Now, element 101 is named Mendelevium after him.

His name is pronounced 'Men-de-LAY-ev'.

Today, we know there is a whole lot more out there than just our Solar System – a mindbogglingly large Universe, with billions of galaxies, each made of billions of stars and planets. So what is the Universe made of? Surprise – while our Solar System and other stars and planets are made of atoms, most of the stuff in the Universe is not; it is made of very strange stuff – dark matter and dark energy – that we do not understand as well as we understand atoms.

Did you know?

In the Universe as a whole, atoms account for around 5% of what's there, and dark matter for approximately 27%, while dark energy comes in at about 68%.

Only about one in ten of those atoms is in the form of stars, planets or living things, with the rest probably existing in a gaseous form too hot to have made stars and planets.

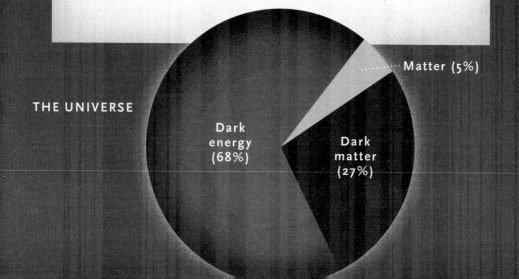

THE UNIVERSE

Matter (5%)

Dark energy (68%)

Dark matter (27%)

Dark Matter and Dark Energy

Dark Matter

Let's begin with dark matter.

How do we know it is there? What is it? And how come we don't find it on Earth or even in our Sun?

We know it is there because the force of its gravity holds together our Galaxy, the Andromeda Galaxy and all the other big structures in the Universe. The visible part of the Andromeda Galaxy, and all other galaxies, sits in the middle of an enormous sphere of dark matter (it's ten times larger than the galaxies, and astronomers call it the dark halo).

Without the gravity of the dark matter, most of the stars, solar systems and everything else in the galaxies would go flying off into space, which would be a very bad thing.

At the moment, we don't know exactly what the dark matter is made of (not unlike Democritus, who had an idea – atoms – but didn't have the details). But here is what we do know.

Dark matter particles are not made of the same particles that atoms are (protons, neutrons and electrons); it is a new form of matter! Don't be too surprised – it took nearly 200 years to identify all the different kinds of atoms, and over the course of time, many new forms of atomic matter were discovered.

Because dark matter is not made of the same material as atoms, it is pretty much oblivious to atoms (and vice versa). Moreover, dark matter particles are oblivious to other dark matter particles. A physicist would say that dark matter particles interact with atoms and with themselves very weakly, if at all. Because of this fact, when our Galaxy and other galaxies formed, the dark matter remained in the very large and diffuse dark matter halo, while the atoms collided with one another and sank to the centre of the dark halo, eventually forming stars and planets made almost completely of atoms.

The 'shyness' of dark matter particles, then, is why stars, planets and all living things are made of atoms and not of dark matter.

Nonetheless, dark matter particles are buzzing around

our neighbourhood – at any given time scientists think there is about one dark matter particle in a good-sized teacup. And this is key to testing this bold idea. Dark matter particles are shy, but can occasionally leave a telltale signature in a very, very sensitive particle detector. For this reason, physicists have built large detectors and placed them underground (to shield them from the cosmic rays that bombard the surface of the Earth) to see if dark matter particles really do make up our halo.

Even more exciting is creating new dark matter particles at a particle accelerator by turning energy into mass, according to Einstein's famous formula, $E = mc^2$.

The Large Hadron Collider in Geneva, Switzerland, the most powerful particle accelerator ever built, is trying to create and detect dark matter particles.

You can find out more about the LHC on page 95.

Satellites in the sky are looking for pieces of atoms that are created when dark matter particles in the halo occasionally collide and produce ordinary matter (the reverse of what particle accelerators are trying to do).

If one or more of these methods is successful, we will be able to confirm that something other than atoms makes up the bulk of the matter in the Universe. Wow!

And now we are ready to talk about the biggest mystery in all science: dark energy.

This is such a big puzzle that solving it might even topple Einstein's theory of gravity, general relativity!

Dark Energy

We all know that the Universe is expanding, having grown in size for the past 13.8 billion years after the Big Bang. Since Edwin Hubble discovered the expansion more than 80 years ago, astronomers have been trying to measure the slowing of the expansion due to gravity. Gravity is the force that holds us to the Earth, keeps all the planets orbiting the Sun, and is generally nature's cosmic glue. Gravity is an attractive force – it pulls things together and slows down everything from balls to rockets that are launched from Earth – and so the expansion of the Universe should be slowing down due to all the stuff attracting all the other stuff.

In 1998, astronomers discovered that this simple but very logical idea couldn't be more wrong. They discovered that the expansion of the Universe is not slowing down, but instead it is speeding up. (They did this by using the time-machine aspect of telescopes: because light takes time to travel from across the Universe to us, when we look at distant objects we see them as they were long ago. Using powerful telescopes, including the Hubble Space Telescope, they were able to determine that the Universe was expanding more slowly long ago.)

How can this be? According to Einstein's theory, some stuff – stuff even weirder than dark matter – has repulsive gravity. ('Repulsive gravity' means gravity that pushes things apart rather than pulling them together, which is very strange indeed!) It goes by the name of 'dark energy' and could be something as simple as the energy of quantum nothingness, or as weird as the influence of additional space–time dimensions! Or there may be no dark energy at all, and we need to replace Einstein's theory of general relativity with something better.

Part of what makes dark energy such an important puzzle is the fact that it holds the fate of the Universe in its hands. Right now, dark energy is stepping on the accelerator and the expansion of the Universe is speeding up, suggesting that it will expand forever, with the sky returning to darkness in about 100 billion years.

Since we don't understand dark energy, we can't rule out the possibility that it will put its foot on the brake at some time in the future, perhaps even causing the Universe to collapse.

These are all challenges for the scientists of the future – you, maybe? – to explore and understand.

What You Need to Need to Know About Black Holes

Professor STEPHEN HAWKING

What is a black hole?

A black hole is a region where gravity is so strong that any light that tries to escape gets dragged back. Because nothing can travel faster than light, everything else will get dragged back too. So if you fell into a black hole you'd never get out again. A black hole has always been thought of as the ultimate prison from which there's no escape. Falling into a black hole is like falling over Niagara Falls: there's no way of getting back out the same way you came in.

The edge of a black hole is called the 'horizon'. It is like the edge of a waterfall. If you are above the edge, you can get away if you paddle fast enough, but once you pass the edge, you are doomed.

As more things fall into a black hole, it gets bigger and the horizon moves further out. It is like feeding a pig. The more you feed it, the larger it gets.

How is a black hole made?

To make a black hole, you need to squash a very large amount of matter into a very small space. Then the pull of gravity will be so strong that light will be dragged back, unable to escape.

Scientists think that one way black holes are formed is when stars that have burned up their fuel explode like giant hydrogen bombs. These explosions are called supernovas. The explosion will drive off the outer layers of the star in a great expanding shell of gas and it will push the central regions inwards. If the star is big enough (at least three times the size of our Sun), a black hole will form.

Much larger black holes are formed inside clusters and at the centre of galaxies. These regions will contain black holes and neutron stars as well as ordinary stars. Collisions between black holes and the other objects will produce a growing black hole that swallows anything that comes too close. Our Galaxy, the Milky Way, has a black hole several million times the mass of our Sun at its centre.

Neutron Stars

When massive stars run out of fuel, they usually expel all their outer layers in a giant explosion called a supernova. Such an explosion is so powerful and bright it can outshine the light of billions and billions of stars put together.

But sometimes not everything is expelled in such an explosion. Sometimes the core of the star can remain behind as a ball. After a supernova explosion, this remnant is very hot: around 100,000°C (180,000°F), but there is no more nuclear reaction to keep it hot.

Some remnants are so massive that under the influence of gravity they collapse in on themselves until they are only a few dozen kilometres – miles – across. For this to happen, these remnants need to have a mass that is between around 1.4 and 2.1 times the mass of the Sun.

The pressure is so intense inside these balls that they become liquid inside, surrounded by a solid crust about 1.6 km (1 mile) thick. The liquid is made of particles that normally remain inside the core of the atoms – the neutrons – so these balls are called neutron stars.

There are also other particles inside neutron stars, but they really consist mostly of neutrons. To create such a liquid on Earth is beyond our present technology.

Many neutron stars have been observed by modern telescopes. Since the cores of stars are made of the heaviest elements forged inside stars (like iron), they are extremely heavy (about the mass of the Sun).

Remnants more massive than 2.1 times the size of the Sun never stop collapsing on themselves and become black holes.

Stars Like the Sun

Stars like the Sun do not explode in supernovas but become red giants, whose remnants are not massive enough to shrink under their own gravity. Some outside layers are dispersed into space. The inner core will cool and shrink. These inner remnants are called white dwarfs.

Star remnants that are less heavy than 1.4 times the mass of the Sun become white dwarfs, although white dwarfs can be quite small (about the size of the Earth).

White dwarfs cool down over a period of billions of years, until they are not hot any more.

How can you see a black hole?

Until very recently the answer was you couldn't! No light can get out of a black hole. It was like looking for a black cat in a black cellar. Scientists detected a black hole by the way its gravity pulled on other things. They saw stars that were orbiting something they couldn't see, but which they knew could only be a black hole. They also saw discs of gas and dust rotating about a central object they couldn't see, but which they knew could only be a black hole.

The First Picture

Then, in April 2019, the Event Horizon Telescope provided the first photo of a black hole! The team behind the telescope included 29-year-old Katherine Bouman, who wrote one of the key algorithms that resulted in the first black-hole photo. The supermassive black hole pictured is at the core of the enormous galaxy Messier 87. It looks rather like a luminous fuzzy ring doughnut on a black background.

The Event Horizon Telescope

The Event Horizon Telescope isn't a single instrument. It is a series of radio telescopes, positioned all around the world. Different countries came together to set it up in 2009. Now there are 20, and more countries are joining. Working together, these telescopes can make an aperture that is equal to the diameter of the entire Earth.

The Milky Way is another name for the galaxy that
contains our Solar System – so called because of the
hazy, 'milky' band of light we can see from Earth.
Find out more about our galaxy on page 5:
A Voyage Across the Universe.

How would it feel to visit an erupting volcano?
Find out on page 81.

In 1969 Neil Armstrong and Buzz Aldrin became the first humans to set foot on the Moon.

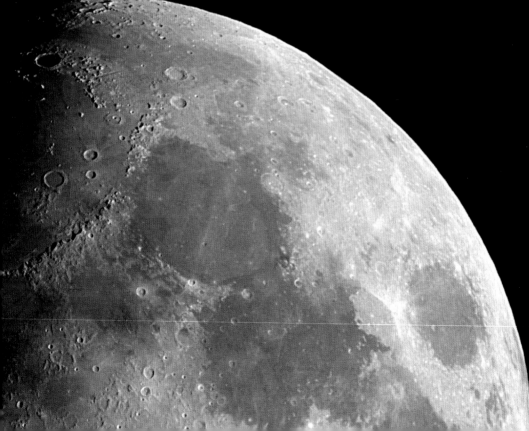

THE BLUE MARBLE
The first photograph taken of our
Earth from the surface of the Moon.
Find out more about Neil and
Buzz's journey on page 243.

The Kármán line is the boundary between
Earth's atmosphere and outer space.
Read more on page 124.

A model of our Solar System, which shows the planets, in order, moving away from the Sun: Mercury, Venus, Earth, Mars, Jupiter, Saturn, Uranus, Neptune.

The surface of our neighbouring planet. Mars is cold and rocky, with a thin atmosphere made mostly of carbon dioxide.

Find out more on page 150.

Discover the secret behind
Saturn's rings on page 163.

The Andromeda Galaxy is the closest
large galaxy to our own Milky Way.
You can read about it on page 176.

Alpha Centauri is the closest star system to our Sun.
Find out more on page 172.

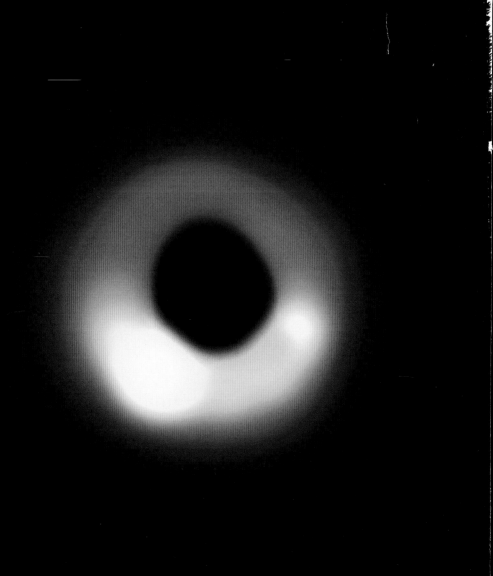

This is a rendered image of what
a black hole looks like to us.
Read Stephen Hawking's essay
about black holes on page 206.

Falling into a Black Hole

You can fall into a black hole just as you can fall into the Sun. If you fall in feet first, your feet will be nearer to the black hole than your head and will be pulled harder by the gravity of the black hole. So you will be stretched out lengthwise and squashed in sideways. This stretching and squeezing is stronger the smaller the black hole is. If you fall into a black hole made by a star only a few times the size of our Sun, you will be torn apart and made into spaghetti before you even reach the black hole. But if you fall into a much bigger black hole, you will pass the horizon – the edge of the black hole and the point of no return – without noticing anything in particular. However, someone watching you fall in from a distance will never see you cross the horizon because gravity warps time and space near a black hole. To them, you will appear to slow down as you approach the horizon and get dimmer and dimmer. You get dimmer because the light you send out takes longer and longer to get away from the black hole. If you cross the horizon at 11:00 according to your wristwatch, someone looking at you would see the watch slow down and never quite reach 11:00.

Getting Out of a Black Hole

People used to think nothing could ever get out of a black hole. After all, that's why they were called black holes! Anything that fell into a black hole was thought to be lost and gone forever; black holes would last until the end of time. They were eternal prisons from which there was no hope of escape.

But then it was discovered that this picture wasn't quite right. Tiny fluctuations in space and time meant that black holes couldn't be the perfect traps they were once thought to be; instead, they would slowly leak particles in the form of Hawking Radiation. The rate of leakage is slower the bigger the black hole is.

Hawking Radiation causes black holes to evaporate gradually. The rate of evaporation will be very slow at first but it will speed up as the black hole gets smaller. Eventually, after billions and billions of years, the black hole will disappear. So black holes aren't eternal prisons after all. But what about their prisoners – the things that made the black hole or that fell in later? They will be recycled into energy and particles. But if you examine what comes out of the black hole very carefully, you can reconstruct what was inside. So the memory of what falls into a black hole is not lost forever, just for a very long time.

You *can* get out of a black hole!

Singularities

singularity is a place where the mathematics used by physicists goes horribly wrong! For example, as you approach the centre of a black hole – one type of singularity – space-time curvature grows to infinity and the normal rules of mathematics fail at the exact centre (they say to divide by zero, which everyone knows isn't allowed!).

Sometimes a physics calculation makes an assumption which turns out to be wrong at a particular point, and a singularity is found. Once this is understood, the calculation can be adapted so that the error is fixed, the maths works properly, and the singularity disappears. Result!

The more interesting singularities are harder to get rid of and suggest that a new theory is needed. For example, black hole and Big Bang singularities occur in the maths of general relativity. Perhaps a theory with very different maths is needed to understand what is really going on, and to get sensible results at such places in the Universe.

This is a busy area of research for scientists who hope that a Theory of Everything will get rid of these singularities.

The Big Bang

The space–time curvature becomes
infinite
the density of matter becomes
infinite
the temperature becomes
infinite
the space containing all we see around us in the Universe
reaches zero size
and all paths going back in time come . . .
to an end.

This singularity is also known as an initial singularity because it sits at the beginning of time.

Going Dark

What Would Happen If the Lights Went Out

What would it be like if all the lights suddenly went out? Can you imagine living in darkness because there was no more electricity? Imagine if you had to go to bed when the Sun went down – in some parts of the world, you would be tucked up by 4.00 p.m. in the winter! Astronomers might be thrilled that a lack of electric light would mean no light pollution spoiling their view of the night sky – but they might find day-to-day life a bit more tricky than usual!

Why We Might Lose Power

There are all sorts of reasons why a huge power cut could strike the Earth.

- Terrorist acts – or events in a war – could knock out power stations.
- We are likely to face problems with supplies as more and more people on Earth want to use lots and lots of electricity.
- Already bad weather on Earth regularly causes thousands of homes to lose their power supply.

The Importance of the Sun

But it's not just Earth weather that could make your home go dark – experts now think that space weather could drastically affect our electricity supply over the next few years. We get most of our light, of course, from our Sun. But the Sun can also disturb our weather. A coronal mass ejection (CME) – when the Sun throws out a great bolt of solar matter and energy – can cause magnetic storms or a rise in radiation levels. These can disrupt electrical power grids and radio communications on Earth.

CMEs happen most often during a solar maximum – the time of greatest solar activity during the Sun's 11-year cycle. Scientists who study the Sun believe that the Earth was in a solar maximum between 2013 and 2015. This was great for viewing the Northern Lights, a spectacular night-time show of coloured lights in the northern sky, caused by electrons and protons from the solar wind interacting with gas in the atmosphere. But the solar maximum always has potential to cause problems on Earth with our power supplies.

So . . . what might life be like if the lights went out?

Light

Human beings existed on the Earth long before the invention of the electric light bulb! So we should be fine without electric light. We could light our homes with candles or lamps.

Modern technology has also provided us with battery or solar-powered lamps which we could use in a power cut. But we would have far less light than we are used to once the Sun has set. And we would have to be careful not to run down our supplies, especially if we had no idea how long the power cut might last.

Heat

Many of us rely on electricity for warmth. Even people with gas boilers, which need electricity to ignite, would find themselves with no heat in their homes. Many of us use electricity to cook – so we'd have to think again about how to make a hot meal. And keeping food fresh, even in cold temperatures, would become a challenge without a working fridge or freezer. With a wood-burning stove and plenty of logs, we could huddle around it to keep warm. We would have to wear more clothes and go to bed much earlier.

Water

You might not have any water at all! And even if you did still have running water, very quickly that water would not be clean enough to drink. Without electricity, our vast water purification plants and sewage plants would stop working. So you would have to filter and then boil water before it was pure enough to drink. You would have to heat water to wash yourself and your clothes – which you would have to do by hand as machines wouldn't be working.

Entertainment

We could play Scrabble (the board game, not the online version) by torchlight, wearing our winter coats, sitting round a wood or coal fire in the evenings, eating food that we'd heated up over the fire! But we wouldn't be able to watch television or play computer games. Your mobile phone would lose its charge quite fast, unless you have a solar-powered charger. You might be able to use the landline as the telephone system works off a different grid to mains electricity. And if you had a wind-up radio, you could listen to it, which would be a good way of getting news and updates.

Did you know that there was once a TV powered by a bicycle in a science museum in Bristol? The faster you pedalled, the better the picture on the TV. Would you want to have a go?

Life without electricity would be very different for most people on Earth! How do you think your life would change if electricity didn't flow at the flick of a switch?

Black Holes

SASHA HACO

Astrophysicist, University of Cambridge

Gravity acts between any two objects, between the ground and your feet, between your body and this book, and even between the pages of this book! The strength of the gravity depends on how massive the objects are. The pages of this book are so light that the gravity between them is unnoticeably tiny. But when there are objects as big as the Earth or the Sun, we start to feel the effects of gravity. The gravity between the Sun and the Earth is what keeps the Earth in its orbit round the Sun. It is the gravitational pull of the Earth that keeps us obediently fixed on its surface – if we jump up in the air, we always come back down again. If we throw a ball up into the air, it also falls back down.

But if we throw it hard enough (really, really hard!), it will travel so fast as to escape from the Earth's gravity and never return. This is how we can get rockets to the Moon – we have to launch them extremely fast into space.

There is a special speed required for an object to leave the Earth's gravity, called the escape velocity. It is dependent on the mass of the Earth: objects more massive than the Earth have a higher escape velocity – we'd have to launch the rocket even faster in order to stop it falling back down. When the object is really huge, so that the gravity is extremely strong, the escape velocity can reach the speed of light. Nothing can travel faster than the speed of light – it is our universal speed limit. This means that nothing, not even light, can escape from these enormous objects – they suck in everything around them. These massive objects are called black holes. The distance all around the black hole at which light gets 'too close' and so gets pulled in is called the event horizon of the black hole. So, in a way, the name 'black hole' is a bit strange: it isn't really a hole at all, it is actually full of a huge amount of matter!

What do black holes look like?

We see things by light bouncing off them and entering our eyes. But the problem is, light can't bounce off black holes, because as soon as the light crosses the event horizon, it gets sucked in and doesn't come out. This means that we can't directly see black holes! And this is the reason that black holes have their name – it's because, to us, they just look like black empty space.

If we can't see black holes, how can we know they exist?

As explained earlier by Stephen Hawking, we can detect the presence of black holes by looking at how objects move round them. The huge tug of the black hole's gravity means that objects (such as stars close by) travel along different paths than they would if the black hole wasn't there. We can observe how these stars move, and detect that there must be a black hole nearby even if we cannot directly see it. This indirect evidence has meant that some people questioned the existence of black holes – until a few years ago. There has been a major development since Hawking's original essay: black holes can now be observed directly!

About 1.3 billion years ago (that's 1,300,000,000 years ago!) two black holes collided with each other. This resulted in an enormous explosion, sending shock waves hurtling outwards into space. Just as when you drop a pebble into a pond you can watch how the water ripples outwards, these gravitational waves rippled outwards from the black holes, and have been travelling through the Universe ever since. On 14 September 2015, these waves finally passed by Earth and created a tiny ripple in space. This minute change was picked up by a detector in the United States, telling us about this extraordinary event all those years ago. So, as of 2015, we have direct evidence of black holes.

Our ability to observe black holes became even more exciting only recently in 2019, when an image of a black hole was produced. The image shows a dark circle surrounded by a bright halo of light. The bright ring is caused by light bending from the extreme gravity close to the black hole. The dark circle is a huge black hole, one that is bigger than the size of our entire Solar System. It took eight telescopes on Earth, all working together, to produce this image, and it is a remarkable achievement.

Can anything get out of a black hole?

Stephen Hawking wrote in his earlier essay that even though black holes pull everything in, there is the possibility that they also 'slowly leak particles in the form of Hawking Radiation'. This was one of Hawking's greatest discoveries. Over time, energy leaks from the black hole in the form of this radiation. This means that if we wait long enough, a black hole will evaporate. The idea of black holes evaporating has caused a huge amount of debate among scientists. Eventually, once the black hole has evaporated, there will be nothing left but empty space. But what happened to all the stuff that falls in? Hawking explained in his chapter that everything that falls in is contained within this Hawking Radiation. He says: 'So black holes aren't eternal prisons after all . . . the memory of what falls into a black hole is not lost forever, just for a very long time.' This is actually rather controversial! The problem is, no one knows this for sure. It was just Hawking's inspired thinking. For the last decade of his life, Hawking worked extremely hard to show that this is true. He published some famous papers over his last few years, making great progress to explain what happens to all the information about everything that originally made up the black hole. Nothing is proven yet, but it's looking likely that Hawking was right.

Part Five

Life in Space

Why Do We Go Into Space?

Professor STEPHEN HAWKING

Why do we go into space? Why go to all that effort and spend all that money just for a few lumps of moon rock? Aren't there better things we could be doing here on Earth?

But spreading out into space will have an incredible effect. It will completely change the future of the human race. It could decide whether we have a future at all.

It won't solve any of our immediate problems on Planet Earth, but it will help us look at them in a different way. The time has come when we need to look outwards across the Universe rather than inwards at ourselves on an increasingly overcrowded planet.

Moving the human race out into space won't happen quickly. By that, I mean it could take hundreds, or even thousands, of years. We could have a base on the Moon within 30 years, reach Mars in 50 years, and explore the moons of the outer planets in 200 years. By reach, I mean with manned – or should I say personed? – flight. We have already driven rovers on Mars and landed a probe on Titan, a moon of Saturn, but when we're dealing with the future of the human race, we have to go there ourselves and not just send robots.

But go where? Now that astronauts have lived for months on the International Space Station, we know that human beings can survive away from Planet Earth. But we also know that living in zero gravity on the space station doesn't only make it difficult to have a cup of tea! It's not very good for people to live in zero gravity for a long time, so if we're to have a base in space we need it to be on a planet or moon.

Zero Gravity

Zero gravity is a term often used to describe a condition of weightlessness. Being weightless for any length of time can affect people's health. Some people suffer from space sickness (this includes being sick, feeling dizzy and having headaches), though this doesn't last longer than 3 days at most. Muscles can waste away, so astronauts all exercise when in space for any length of time. Blood flow slows down, and body fluids are redistributed so astronauts' faces look puffy: a condition called 'moon-face'. These changes all disappear quickly when astronauts return to Earth.

So which one shall we choose? The most obvious is the Moon. It is close, and quite easy to get to. We've already landed on it, and driven across it in a buggy. On the other hand, the Moon is small, and without an atmosphere or a magnetic field to deflect solar wind particles, like on Earth. There is no liquid water, but there may be ice in the craters at the north and south poles. A colony on the Moon could use this as a source of oxygen and water, with power provided by nuclear energy or solar panels. The Moon could be a base for travel to the rest of the Solar System.

What about Mars? That's our next obvious target. Mars is further from the Sun than Planet Earth is, so it gets less warmth from the sunlight, making temperatures much colder. Once, Mars had a magnetic field, but that decayed 4 billion years ago, meaning that it was stripped of most of its atmosphere, leaving it with only 1% of the pressure of the Earth's atmosphere.

In the past, the atmospheric pressure – the weight of the air above you in the atmosphere – must have been higher because we can see what appear to be dried-up channels and lakes. Liquid water cannot exist on Mars now as it would just evaporate.

But there is lots of water in the form of ice at the two poles. If we went to live on Mars, we could use this. We could also use the minerals and metals that volcanoes have brought to the surface.

So the Moon and Mars might be quite good for us. But where else could we go in the Solar System? Mercury and Venus are far too hot, while Jupiter and Saturn are gas giants, with no solid surface.

We could try the moons of Mars, but they are very small. Some of the moons of Jupiter and Saturn might be better. Titan, a moon of Saturn, is larger and more massive than our Moon, and has a dense atmosphere. The Cassini-Huygens mission of NASA and ESA, the European Space Agency, has landed

Find out more about Titan on page 159.

a probe on Titan, which sent back pictures of the surface. However, it is very cold, being so far from the Sun, and I wouldn't fancy living next to a lake of liquid methane!

What about beyond our Solar System? From looking across the Universe, we know that quite a few stars have planets in orbit round them. Until recently we could see only giant planets the size of Jupiter or Saturn. But now we are starting to spot smaller Earth-like planets too. Some of these will lie in the Goldilocks Zone, where their distance from their home star is in the right range for liquid water to exist on their surface. There are maybe a thousand stars within 10 light years of Earth. If even 1% of these have an Earth-sized planet in the Goldilocks Zone, we have ten candidate new worlds.

Remember the Goldilocks Zone, where things are 'just right'? If not, go to page 66 to refresh your memory!

At the moment we can't travel very far across the Universe. In fact, we can't even imagine how we might be able to cover such huge distances. But that's what we should be aiming to do in the future, over the next 200 to 500 years. The human race has existed as a separate species for about 2 million years. Civilization began about 10,000 years ago, and the rate of development has been steadily increasing. We have now reached the stage where we can boldly go where no one has gone before. And who knows what we will find and who we will meet?

Life on Mars — For Real?

What does this mean for the existence of Martians?

NASA scientists revealed that on Mars in the summer months water flows down canyons and crater walls before drying up in the cooler autumn temperatures. We don't yet know where this water comes from – perhaps it rises up from the ground or maybe it condenses from the thin Martian atmosphere. But excitingly this takes our journey of discovery to find life in the Solar System onward by another step.

Where there is liquid water, scientists think we will find life!

Our Future Colonies

This discovery also means that it might be much easier to found a colony of human life on Mars! If water could be collected from a local supply that would solve one major headache for future missions to the red planet.

Life on Mars just got a step closer!

Building Rockets for Mars

ALLYSON THOMAS

Aerospace Engineer, NASA

When I was growing up, I was interested in maths and science, but my passion was actually ballet. When I was in high school, I enrolled in a very challenging curriculum for maths and science – it had a heavy workload that made it nearly impossible to dedicate the time required to study ballet. But I still wanted to do both! After a difficult year I chose a curriculum that allowed me the flexibility to study ballet too. It was a fantastic decision, because I was able to continue dancing while still preparing myself to study engineering at university.

Now I work at NASA, but I still practise and perform ballet on nights and weekends, so I enjoy the best of both worlds!

As a NASA engineer, I am helping develop the Space Launch System (SLS) rocket that will eventually travel to Mars. This is so exciting, to be part of this great project.

Right now, NASA is preparing to launch Artemis 1, the second planned flight of the Orion Multi-Purpose Crew Vehicle, on a mission to orbit the Moon. NASA hopes to use the SLS for the launch. It is my responsibility to ensure that a part of the rocket called the volume isolator is properly designed for the loads and conditions of this flight.

Volume isolators are used in rockets to contain purge gases within certain sections. These purge gases keep each section at the right temperature and humidity conditions for the sensitive instrumentation inside. This is important because the rocket has cryogenic fuel – this makes it very cold in places, but instrumentation nearby needs to be warmer in order to function properly.

The Artemis programme was originally called Exploration Mission-1 (EM-1). The name was changed in 2019.

The volume isolator I am responsible for is called the MSA diaphragm. It is located near the top of the rocket, just below the crew vehicle in a section of the rocket called the Multi-Purpose Crew Vehicle Stage Adapter, or the MSA for short. It is located there to make sure that the environment

below the isolator
is properly conditioned
by the purge gas.

The MSA diaphragm will
need to endure the force of
lift-off, so it needs to be strong.

But it also needs to be as lightweight as possible to reduce the amount
of fuel needed to launch the crew vehicle into
outer space.

A challenge, right?

Here's how we deal with that.

The MSA diaphragm is dome-shaped, with
a 5 m (16.4 ft) diameter, and it is made from a
high-strength and lightweight material called
carbon composite.

Carbon composite is created by layering
pieces of carbon fabric with epoxy glue. In
the case of the MSA diaphragm, the layers
of carbon fabric are placed inside a large
bowl-shaped mould. Each layer of fabric is laid down at a
different angle in order to create a final product that has
quasi-isotropic properties. This means that the dome will
have the same strength no matter the orientation – this is
important. If the angle of the fabric stayed the same in each
layer, the final product would be strong in one orientation,
but comparatively weak in any other orientation.

After every layer of the MSA diaphragm has been placed

in the mould, the entire mould is rolled into an enormous oven to cure and harden. Once the MSA diaphragm has hardened, it is pried from the mould and machined to add bolt holes that will be used to connect it to the MSA.

This method of creating a strong yet lightweight structure by layering fabric is also used when creating the shoes that allow me as a ballet dancer to dance on my toes! Each shoe is designed with a strong yet lightweight box that surrounds my toes and provides the support needed to balance, spin and even jump on the very tips of my toes. This box is created by layering fabric and glue, much like in the MSA diaphragm.

Not everyone who looks at a rocket part sees a ballet shoe, but my life experiences have given me the perspective to see the world in a unique way. Through following your passions in life, you will begin to see the world from your own unique viewpoint.

At NASA, we aim to build teams of people who have unique perspectives so that we can see problems from multiple angles. This diversity helps us to overcome the many challenges associated with building a rocket – a rocket that will travel all the way to Mars.

Imagining a Life on Mars

KELLIE GERARDI

Space Industry Professional

Mars Astronaut

Normally I enjoy sleeping late, but every year on the morning of my birthday, my eyes seem to pop right open with excitement. Last year was no different, and on the morning of 16 February, I jumped out of bed. Except something *was* different. There were no birds chirping outside my window, no scent of my favourite breakfast wafting in from the kitchen, and I couldn't hear the familiar sounds of my family moving around downstairs.

Then I remembered that I wasn't at home for my birthday this year. In fact, I wasn't even on Planet Earth! I was on Mars with six other scientists from around the world, studying what it's like to live on another planet.

Have you ever wondered what it would be like to live on another world? It's easy to forget that Earth is not the only planet in the Solar System. Seven other planets whiz round the Sun just like we do! This is lucky for us, because some day humans might need to find a new home. We haven't always taken very good care of our planet, and one day the Earth will be overheated and unable to support us. Besides global warming, we also have to remember the dinosaurs! Those magnificent creatures ruled the planet for over 165 million years, until an asteroid struck Earth and ruined their home, driving the dinosaurs to extinction. Today we have special software to track asteroids from far away, but if we want the human species to survive for a million years, we need to spread out and learn how to live in space.

But we can't live just anywhere! We need to find a planet that's not too hot and close to the Sun, like Venus or Mercury, and not too cold and far away, like Uranus or Neptune, and it can't be made of gas like Jupiter and Saturn! That leaves Mars – our rocky red neighbouring planet. Lots of astronauts have visited space, but except for a few short trips to the Moon, they've never been far from Earth. No human has ever travelled to Mars, but we're now starting to prepare for this trip. Imagine a car ride that lasts for more than 200 days with no rest stops. That's how long it would take a crew of astronauts to travel to Mars, 225 million km (140 million miles), or 1.4 AU, away from Earth! When you're that far away from home, no one can send you extra food or water, so you have to bring as much as you can with you, and learn to produce the rest yourself.

Before we send astronauts on such a big journey, we need to understand as many of the challenges they might face as possible. One way we research what life will be like on Mars is by living and working in Martian research stations right here on Earth. These special laboratories, or 'habitats', are designed to look and feel exactly like a house on Mars, with a kitchen, a bathroom, a 'greenhab' to grow food, a laboratory with microscopes and other science tools, and tiny bedrooms for crew members. On the morning of my twenty-sixth birthday, that's exactly where I woke up.

Usually my birthday would be filled with phone calls from friends and hugs from family, but there are no phone calls on Mars, because the signal would take too long to reach Earth! When we want to speak to our families, we can send an email over the internet, but it can still take more than 20 minutes for the message to reach them. That also means we can't watch TV. Instead, we can store digital versions of our favourite books, movies and television programmes on a small computer to read or watch whenever we're bored.

There's almost no time for boredom, though. There's a lot to be done every day, like checking and cleaning equipment, growing crops like potatoes, cooking for the crew, recording videos for students and classrooms, and even venturing outside to collect samples of soil and rocks. Mars doesn't have nearly as much oxygen as Earth, so you need a spacesuit to help you breathe whenever you go outside. When you come back, sticky and sweaty from a long walk in a heavy spacesuit, you can't even take a shower! Water is a precious resource on Mars, and we have to save as much as possible. Instead of taking showers, we clean our bodies with baby wipes!

Baby Wipes

Baby wipes, or wet wipes, are pieces of cloth moistened with liquids such as water and some forms of alcohol. They usually also contain chemicals that stop fungus or bacteria growing on them. They can be kept in packets until they are needed. Though many companies still use plastics to make wet wipes, biodegradable (planet-friendly!) wet wipes are gradually becoming more popular.

My six crewmates must have known that I would miss my family on my birthday, because when I came out from my room, they were waiting with a handmade birthday card. Instead of '26', the card said '13.8', because that's how old I would be on Mars, where years are almost twice as long as Earth-years! They also cooked me a special breakfast of heart-shaped pancakes. Meals can get very boring on Mars. Because fresh food would go rotten quickly, almost all of the food is in a powdered form that you mix with water – even the meat! My favourite Martian meal is macaroni cheese.

I thanked all of my crewmates for such a nice birthday surprise, and I realized that I'm lucky to have such great friends here. Getting along with your crew is very important, especially when you're stuck in a small space together for a long time!

After 3 weeks of living and working in a Mars habitat, I know life won't be easy for the first astronauts who travel there. I would miss all of my friends and family, my favourite foods, warm showers, and even just being able to breathe fresh air outside without a helmet on. Still, I would choose to go, and I'm lucky to have a family who encourages me to reach for the stars. We might be years away from the first flight, but I know we'll see footprints on Mars in our lifetime. I certainly hope they're mine!

But even if they're not, I'll always remember a birthday that was out of this world. Maybe you too will one day spend a birthday of yours in a Mars habitat – or even on the distant red planet itself.

Humans in Space

'The Eagle has landed!'

This is the message US astronaut Neil Armstrong radioed back from the Moon to mission control in Houston, Texas, USA, on 20 July 1969. The Eagle was the lunar module, which had detached from the spacecraft Columbia, in orbit 96.5 km (60 miles) above the surface of the Moon. While astronaut Michael Collins remained on board Columbia, the Lunar Excursion Module touched down on an area called the Sea of Tranquility – but there is no water on the Moon so it didn't land with a splash! Neil Armstrong and Buzz Aldrin, the two astronauts inside the Eagle, became the first human beings ever to visit the Moon.

Astronaut Armstrong was the first to step out of the capsule on to the Moon (with his left foot). Buzz Aldrin followed him and looked around – at the totally black sky, the impact craters, the layers of moondust – and commented: 'Magnificent desolation.' As they'd been instructed, they quickly put moon rocks and dust into their pockets, so that they would have some samples of the Moon, even if they had to leave in a hurry.

In fact, they stayed for nearly a day on the Moon and covered nearly a kilometre (0.6 miles) on foot. This epic voyage of Apollo 11 remains one of the most inspirational journeys into the unknown that mankind has ever undertaken, and three craters to the north of the Sea of Tranquility are now named after the astronauts on the mission – Collins, Armstrong and Aldrin.

Walking on the Moon

Including Apollo 11, a total of 12 astronauts have now walked on the Moon. But each mission was still a dangerous business, as was clearly shown on the Apollo 13 mission in April 1970 when an explosion on board the service module meant that not only the astronauts but also the people on the ground had to make heroic efforts to return the space-craft safely to Earth.

Astronauts are highly trained specialists with backgrounds in aviation, engineering and science. But to launch and operate a space mission needs people with a wide variety of skills. The Apollo missions – like all space missions before and since – were the result of work by tens of thousands of people who built and operated the complex hardware and software.

The Apollo missions also brought back 381 kg (840 lb) of lunar material, like moon rock, to be studied on Earth. This allowed scientists on our planet to gain a much better understanding of the Moon and how it relates to the Earth.

The last mission to the Moon was Apollo 17, which landed on the Taurus-Littrow highlands on 11 December 1972 and stayed for 3 days. When they were 29,000 km (18,000 miles) from the Earth on their way to the Moon, the Apollo 17 crew took a photo of the complete Earth, fully lit. This photo is known as 'the Blue Marble' and may be the most widely distributed photo ever. Since then, no human being has been far enough away from the Earth to take such a picture.

The First Man in Space

The Apollo missions were not the first time that a human had flown into space. Soviet cosmonaut Yuri Gagarin, who orbited the Earth on 12 April 1961 in the Vostok spacecraft, was the first-ever human being in space.

Six weeks after Gagarin's historic achievement, US President John F. Kennedy announced that he wanted to land a man on the Moon within 10 years, and the newly created NASA – the National Aeronautics and Space Administration – set to work to see if they could match the Russian-manned space programme, even though at that time NASA had only 16 minutes of space-flight experience. The space race – to be the first on the Moon – had begun!

Mercury, Gemini — and Walking in Space

Project Mercury, a US single-astronaut programme, was designed to see if human beings could survive in space. In 1961, astronaut Alan Shepard became the first American in space with a suborbital flight of 15 minutes, and the following year John Glenn became the first NASA astronaut to orbit the Earth.

NASA's Project Gemini followed. Gemini was a very important project as it taught astronauts how to dock vehicles in space. It also allowed them to practise operations such as spacewalks, also called EVAs (Extra-Vehicular Activity). But the first spacewalk ever performed was by a Russian cosmonaut, Alexei Leonov, in 1965. The Russians didn't make it to the Moon first, however, with this honour going to the USA in 1969.

The First Space Stations

After the race to land on the Moon was over, many people became less interested in space programmes. However, both the Russians and the Americans still had big plans. The Russians were working on a super-secret programme called Almaz – or Diamond. They wanted to have a manned space station orbiting the Earth. After a doomed first attempt, the next versions, Salyut-3 and then Salyut-5, were more successful but neither of them lasted for much more than a year.

The Americans developed their own version, Skylab – an orbiting space station which was in operation for 8 months in 1973. Skylab had a telescope on board that astronauts used to observe the Sun. They brought back solar photographs including X-ray images of solar flares and dark spots on the Sun.

A Handshake in Space

At this time on Earth – the mid 1970s – both the USSR and the USA were locked into what was known as the Cold War. This meant the two sides were not actually fighting a war but they disliked and distrusted each other very strongly. However, in space the two countries began to work together. In 1975, the Apollo–Soyuz project saw the first 'handshake in space' between the two opposing superpowers. Apollo, the US spacecraft, docked with Soyuz, the Soviet one, and the American astronaut and Russian cosmonaut – who would have had difficulty meeting in person on Earth – shook hands with each other.

The Shuttle

The space shuttle was a new type of spacecraft. Unlike the craft that went before it, it was reusable, designed to fly into space like a rocket but also to glide back to Earth and land like an aeroplane on a runway. The shuttle was also designed to take cargo as well as astronauts into space. The first US shuttle to fly in space – Columbia – was launched in 1981. The last flight was made by Atlantis, in July 2011.

The first shuttle of all was Enterprise, which was used for testing but couldn't orbit the Earth.

The International
Space Station

In 1986, the Russians launched the space station Mir, which means World or Peace.

Mir was the first elaborate, large space station ever to orbit the Earth. It was built in space over 10 years and designed as a 'space laboratory' so that scientists could carry out experiments in a nearly gravity-free environment. Mir was about the size of a double-decker bus and was home to between three and six astronauts at a time.

The International Space Station (ISS) was built in space, with its construction beginning in 1998. Orbiting the globe every 90 minutes, this research facility is a symbol of international cooperation with scientists and astronauts from many countries involved both in running it and spending time there. The ISS was serviced by the space shuttle from NASA, the Soyuz spacecraft from Russia and the European Space Agency's Automated Transfer Vehicles. Now only the Russian and European rockets fly there. The crew also have permanent escape vehicles, in case they need to make an emergency exit!

The Overview Effect

An Astronaut's Journey Through Space

Dr RICHARD GARRIOTT DE CAYEUX

ISS Astronaut

think almost everyone dreams of going into space at some point in their lives. Sadly, though, most give up on that dream when they determine that the odds of going seem so small. In my case, however, my father and both my next-door neighbours' fathers were astronauts. In my neighbourhood, it seemed normal to believe that all of us would go into space some day.

When I found out that I did not qualify to be a NASA astronaut, because of my poor eyesight, I decided I must build a private space agency, so that I could fly. I invested the money I earned making computer games in companies that eventually made it possible for me and others to fly to space privately. In October 2008, I flew to the International Space Station and became the first second-generation American astronaut – and I flew with the first second-generation Russian cosmonaut, Sergey Volkov!

Preparing for and making a trip to space is an amazing experience! Many of the details were very different from what I expected, or the impression you get from watching television or movies about space.

Before you fly, you must train to operate the spacecraft. Training was a great deal of fun, and I was amazed that most of it was very similar to activities students do at school, or in some after-school clubs. For example, many people like to scuba dive, as I do. When you get a scuba-diving licence, you learn about air pressure and gases like oxygen and carbon dioxide, expanding on what you learn in school in chemistry and physics. This is almost exactly the same as the life support on board a spacecraft. If you can get a scuba licence, you can operate life support in space! Similarly, if you can get an amateur radio-operator licence on Earth, you can operate the radios on a spacecraft. Learning to be a qualified astronaut was more fun and less difficult than I had imagined . . . as long as you are a good student in school!

Then there is the space flight itself. When you watch a rocket launch into the sky, it is very loud, and you can feel the massive vibration. However, when I launched into space, inside the rocket it was quite the opposite. When the engines lit up, we could barely feel or hear it. When the rocket began to lift off, it was very gentle. I have often described it as feeling like a confident ballet move, lifting us ever faster into the sky. For just over 8 minutes you feel about three times the force of gravity, then the engines cut off . . . and you are floating weightlessly in orbit over Earth.

The view is, of course, spectacular, but I was immediately struck by how close we remained to Earth. Aeroplanes can fly almost 16 km (10 miles) above Earth, and we were orbiting about 25 times higher than that. However, that is still close enough to see many of the same details you see from a plane, yet far enough to see the whole Earth below you.

It is a strange feeling to be both unexpectedly near Earth, but also totally isolated from anyone down there on the surface. You clearly understand that if an emergency arises, you and your crewmates must solve it, for there is little help that can come from the surface. Learning to be both self-reliant and to be a reliable team member is also essential preparation for a space flight, and for life in general!

Many astronauts are deeply moved by seeing the Earth from space. There is even a term called 'the Overview Effect', which refers to how people are changed by this experience of seeing Earth from space. I too experienced this, and I think it is worth sharing.

When orbiting on board the ISS, you are travelling round Earth at about 27,690 km/h (17,210 mph). At that speed you go all the way round our planet about every 90 minutes. That means you see a sunrise or a sunset every 45 minutes, and you cross entire continents in 10–20 minutes. Yet you are close enough to Earth to see clearly more detail than you might expect, even things as small as the Golden Gate Bridge in San Francisco (though you cannot see the Great Wall of China, as many have believed). Looking out of the window at the Earth, seeing it in great detail while it smoothly rolls by, was like having a fire hose of information shooting into your mind about the Earth itself.

One of the first things you notice about the Earth from space is its weather. This is because a large portion of the Earth is always covered by clouds. From space you notice things like how over the Pacific Ocean large smooth or geometric patterns of weather form, as the ocean is free from large islands or surface- temperature variations. On the other hand, the Atlantic Ocean is filled with more chaotic weather patterns. This is because of the highly varied surface temperatures, and shapes of nearby continents that interrupt the smoothness you see in the Pacific.

The next thing I noticed was how beautiful the deserts of the Earth are, as they are generally not covered by clouds. Sand and snow on Earth is blown into small drifts, then bigger dunes, then even bigger ridges, and from space you can see the rolling hills of sands that make similar patterns that scale all the way up to being seen from space! It was amazing to see these 'great fans' caused only by the winds blowing across the deserts of the Earth.

From space, it also became clear how completely humanity now occupies the whole surface of the Earth. Every desert I saw had roads across it, and often farms growing crops with water pumped up from deep within the Earth. Every forest, even in the Amazon basin of Brazil, had roads and cities within it. Every mountain range had roads through passes and dams along its rivers. I saw very little 'open space' left on the Earth.

Finally, I saw an area I knew very well, the area of Texas, USA, I grew up in. I saw my hometown, and nearby towns I had driven to many times, as well as the long Texas coastline where I used to visit beaches. And in the same view I could see the whole Earth, which I had now orbited many times. Suddenly it hit me . . . I now knew the true scale of the Earth by direct observation.

I had a huge physical reaction to this moment! It was like watching a movie, where they might zoom in the camera lens while moving the camera backwards. It creates an effect where the hallway seems to collapse and shorten while the actor stays the same size. It was like that as I looked at the Earth; it remained the same size out of the window, but the reality of scale around it collapsed. Suddenly to me, the Earth, which had been unimaginably large, became finite. . . and, in fact, rather small.

Since my return from space, I have learned that many astronauts express a similar epiphany from this 'Overview Effect'. Many astronauts, including myself, come home with a renewed sense of the importance of environmentalism to protect this fragile world we have. It seems to me that if more people had the chance to see the Earth from space, we would all take better care of our precious planet and of each other.

If space travel is a dream of yours, as it was a dream of mine, I hope you will fulfil it some day. The opportunities to do so are increasing every year. However, space will always be more difficult to reach than the next town, country or continent. You will still have to work hard to earn a place on a team that is expanding human knowledge of and presence in locations ever further from our home planet. You won't have to be as lucky to be selected as many early astronauts were though. Work hard, and I believe each one of you reading this can build your own destiny in space!

The Drake Equation

The Drake Equation isn't really an equation; it's a series of questions that help us to work out how many intelligent civilizations with the ability to communicate there might be in our Galaxy. It was formulated in 1961 by Dr Frank Drake of the SETI Institute, and is still used by scientists today.

This is the Drake Equation:

$$N = N^* \times f_p \times n_e \times f_l \times f_i \times f_c \times L$$

N^* represents the number of new stars born each year in the Milky Way Galaxy.

Question: What is the birth rate of stars in the Milky Way Galaxy?

Answer: Our Galaxy is about 12 billion years old, and contains roughly 300 billion stars. So, on average, stars are born at a rate of 300 billion divided by 12 billion = 25 stars per year.

fp is the fraction of those stars that have planets around them.

> **Q:** What percentage of stars have planetary systems?
>
> **A:** Current estimates range from 20% to 70%.

ne is the number of planets per star that are capable of sustaining life.

> **Q:** For each star that does have a planetary system, how many planets are capable of sustaining life?
>
> **A:** Current estimates range from 0.5 to 5.

fl is the fraction of planets in **ne** where life evolves.

> **Q:** On what percentage of the planets that are capable of sustaining life does life actually evolve?
>
> **A:** Current estimates range from 100% (where life can evolve, it will) down to close to 0%.

fi is the fraction of habitable planets with life where intelligent life evolves.

> **Q:** On the planets where life does evolve, what percentage evolves intelligent life?
>
> **A:** Estimates range from 100% (intelligence has such a survival advantage that it will certainly evolve) down to near 0%.

fc is the fraction of planets with intelligent life capable of interstellar communication.

> **Q:** What percentage of intelligent races have the means and the desire to communicate?
>
> **A:** 10% to 20%.

L is the average number of years that a communicating civilization continues to communicate.

Q: How long do communicating civilizations last?

A: This is the toughest of the questions. If we take Earth as an example, we've been communicating with radio waves for less than 100 years. How long will our civilization continue to communicate with this method? Could we destroy ourselves in a few years, or will we overcome our problems and survive for 10,000 years or more?

When all these variables are multiplied together we come up with:

N, the number of communicating civilizations in the Galaxy.

SETI

SETI stands for the Search for Extraterrestrial Intelligence. The SETI Institute listens for radio waves that might be a message from intelligent beings elsewhere in space. It has also sent radio messages into space on the Pioneer and Voyager space probes.

Zero-Gravity Flights

A zero-gravity flight is a way to experience microgravity, or the same kind of gravitational conditions as the astronauts on the International Space Station! That means being able to push off the ceiling with your feet or throw droplets of water around and see them float!

There is a serious point to zero-gravity flights – NASA and other space agencies use zero-gravity flights to train astronauts so they can be better prepared for their work on the space station.

But in 1994 a man called Peter Diamandis decided to offer flights to ordinary passengers as well. He wanted to open up the space-travel experience to everyone, not just professional astronauts. He has flown lots of famous people on his zero-gravity flights, including the second man on the Moon – Buzz Aldrin – and Stephen Hawking, one of the authors of this book.

When you go on a zero-gravity, or zero-G, flight, your plane doesn't leave the Earth's atmosphere. You don't actually go into space.

When taking a zero-G flight, everyone gets on a normal-looking plane, like the sort of plane you might board to go on holiday. But this plane doesn't fly like a normal plane! Instead, it flies in long curves called parabolas.

What happens is this:

• The aeroplane, flown by special, highly qualified pilots, ascends sharply upward. But then it nosedives back to Earth again.

• While the plane is going 'up and over the hump', it puts you into 'zero gravity'. At that point, you are in freefall, just as you would be inside the International Space Station. It's pretty exciting!

1.8 g

• To get you used to the sensation of weightlessness, the first few parabolas – or curves – that the plane flies over are not too steep. This means you have the feeling of reduced gravity, the same conditions you might experience on Mars or the

Zero gravity

1.8 g

Moon. Mars has 40% of the Earth's gravity, so you can bounce around in big leaps. The Moon has less gravity than Mars and so, on the 'lunar parabola', you can do a press-up with one finger!

- When the plane descends again, you experience 'high-G', strong gravitational forces which pin you to the floor. Lying on the floor, you can't even pick up one finger to move it! As the plane ascends once more, you gently start to float away from the floor again.

During the zero-G parabolas, you experience complete weightlessness. You can do a somersault in the air or walk on the ceiling! These zero-G parabolas are over too quickly – everyone says, 'Again! Again!' But what goes up must come down – and eventually your plane must land and bring you back to Earth once more . . .

Robotic Space Travel

Venera 7

Aspace probe is a robotic spacecraft that scientists send out on a journey across the Solar System in order to gather more information about our cosmic neighbourhood. Robotic space missions aim to answer specific questions such as: 'What does the surface of Venus look like?' or 'Is it windy on Neptune?' or 'What is Jupiter made of?'

While robotic space missions are much less glamorous than manned space flight, they have several big advantages:

- Robots can travel for great distances, going far further and faster than any astronaut. Like manned missions, they need a source of power – most use solar arrays which convert sunlight to energy, but others that are travelling long distances away from the Sun take their own on-board generator. However, robotic spacecraft need far less power than manned missions as they don't need to maintain a comfortable living environment on their journey.
- Robots also don't need supplies of food or water and they don't need oxygen to breathe, making them much smaller and lighter than a manned spacecraft.
- Robots don't get bored or homesick or fall ill on their journey.
- If something goes wrong with a robotic mission, no lives are lost in space.
- Space probes cost far less than manned space flights and robots don't want to come home when their mission ends.

Space probes have opened up the wonders of the Solar System to us, sending back data that has allowed scientists to understand far better how the Solar System was formed and what conditions are like on other planets. While human beings have to date travelled only as far as the Moon – a journey averaging 378,000 km (235,000 miles) – space probes have covered billions of miles and shown us extraordinary and detailed images of the far reaches of the Solar System.

In fact, almost 30 space probes reached the Moon before humankind did! Robotic spacecraft have now been sent to all the other planets in our Solar System, they have caught the dust from a comet's tail, landed on Mars and Venus and travelled out beyond Pluto. Some space probes have even taken information about our planet and the human race with them. Probes Pioneer 10 and 11 carry engraved plaques with the image of a man and a woman on them and also a map, showing where the probe came from. As the Pioneers journey onward into deep space, they may one day encounter an alien civilization!

The Voyager probes took photographs of cities, landscapes and people on Earth with them as well as a recorded greeting in many different Earth languages. In the incredibly unlikely event of these probes being picked up by another civilization, these greetings assure any aliens who manage to decode them that we are a peaceful planet and we wish any other beings in our Universe well.

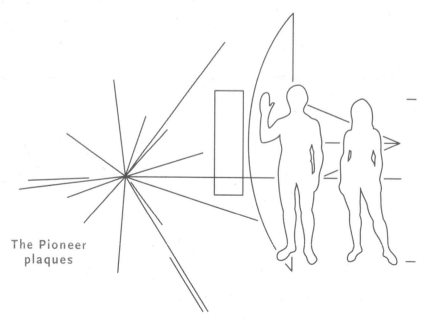

The Pioneer plaques

**Types of
robotic probes**

There are different types of space probes and the type used for a particular mission will depend on the question that the probe is attempting to answer. Some probes fly by planets and take pictures for us, passing by several planets on their long journey[1]. Others orbit a specific planet to gain more information about that planet and its moons[3]. Another type of probe is designed to land and send back data from the surface of another world[2]. Some of these are rovers, others remain fixed wherever they land.

The first rover, Lunokhod 1, was part of a Russian probe, Luna 17, which landed on the Moon in 1970. Lunokhod 1 was a robotic vehicle that could be steered from Earth, in much the same way as a remote-controlled car.

NASA's Mars landers, Viking 1 and Viking 2, which touched down on the red planet in 1976, gave us our first pictures from the surface of the planet of War, which had intrigued people on Earth for millennia. The Viking landers showed the reddish-brown plains, scattered with rocks, the pink sky of Mars and even frost on the ground in winter. Unfortunately, it is very difficult to land on Mars and several probes sent to the red planet have crashed on to the surface.

Later missions to Mars sent the two rovers Spirit and Opportunity. Designed to drive around for at least 3 months, they lasted far longer and also, like other spacecraft sent to Mars, found evidence that Mars had been shaped by the presence of water. In 2007, NASA sent the Phoenix mission to Mars. Phoenix could not drive around Mars but it had a robotic arm to dig into the soil and collect samples. On board, it had a laboratory to examine the soil and work out what it contains. In addition, Mars has several operational orbiters around it – NASA has the Mars Odyssey, Mars Express and Mars Reconnaissance Orbiter, which show us in detail the surface features, and the MAVEN, which studies Mars's atmosphere. Also orbiting Mars are the Mars Orbiter Mission from India, and the ExoMars Trace Gas Orbiter, sent by ESA and Russia.

Curiosity Mars rover

Robotic space probes have also shown us the hellish world that lies beneath the thick atmosphere of Venus. Once it was thought that dense tropical forests might lie under the Venusian clouds but space probes have revealed the high temperatures, heavy carbon-dioxide atmosphere and dark brown clouds of sulphuric acid. In 1990, NASA's Magellan entered orbit round Venus. Using radar to penetrate the atmosphere, Magellan mapped the surface of Venus and found 167 volcanoes larger than 110 km (70 miles) wide! ESA's Venus Express has been in orbit round Venus since 2006. This mission is studying the atmosphere of Venus and trying to find out how Earth and Venus developed in such different ways. The Japanese probe Akatsuki has also, since 2015, been studying the atmosphere of Venus. Several landers, all sent by the former Soviet Union, have returned information from the surface of Venus, a tremendous achievement given the challenges of landing on this most hostile of planets.

In 1970, the Soviet Union's probe Venera 7 was the first man-made object to transmit data from the surface of Venus.

Robotic space probes have braved the scorched world of Mercury, a planet even closer to the Sun than Venus. Mariner 10, which flew by Mercury in 1974 and again in 1975, showed us that this bare little planet looks very similar to our Moon. It is a grey, dead planet with very little atmosphere. In 2008, the MESSENGER mission returned a space probe to Mercury and sent back the first new pictures of the Sun's nearest planet in 30 years.

Flying close to the Sun presents huge challenges for a robotic spacecraft but probes sent to the Sun – Helios 1, Helios 2, SOHO, TRACE, RHESSI and others – have sent back information that helped scientists to develop a far better understanding of the star at the very centre of our Solar System. DISCOVR is currently studying solar winds and coronal mass ejections, and the Parker Solar Probe is on its way. It is due to fly closest to the Sun in 2025.

Further away in the Solar System, Jupiter was first seen in detail when the probe Pioneer 10 flew by in 1973. Pictures captured by Pioneer 10 also showed the Great Red Spot – a feature seen through telescopes from Earth for centuries. After Pioneer, the Voyager probes revealed the surprising news about Jupiter's moons. Thanks to the Voyager probes, scientists on Earth learned that Jupiter's moons are all very different to each other. In 1995, the Galileo probe arrived at Jupiter and spent 8 years investigating the giant gas planet and its moons. Galileo was the first space probe to fly by an asteroid, the first to discover an asteroid with a moon, and the first to measure Jupiter over a long period of time. This amazing space probe also showed the volcanic activity on Jupiter's moon Io and found Europa to be covered in thick ice, beneath which may lie a gigantic ocean that could even harbour some form of life!

NASA's Cassini was not the first to visit Saturn – Pioneer 11 and the Voyager probes had flown past on their long journey and sent back detailed images of Saturn's rings and more information about the thick atmosphere on Titan. But when Cassini arrived in 2004 after a 7-year journey, it showed us many more features of Saturn and the moons that orbit it. Cassini also released a probe, ESA's Huygens, which travelled through the thick atmosphere to land on the surface of Titan. The Huygens probe discovered that Titan's surface is covered in ice and that methane rains down from the dense clouds.

Even further from Earth, Voyager 2 flew by Uranus and showed pictures of this frozen planet tilted on its axis! Thanks to Voyager 2, we also know much more about the thin rings circling Uranus, which are very different to the rings of Saturn, as well as many other details of its moons. Voyager 2 carried on to Neptune and revealed this planet is very windy – Neptune has the fastest-moving storms in the Solar System. In autumn 2019, Voyager 2 was around 11 billion miles from Earth and Voyager 1 was around 14 billion miles away. They should be able to continue communicating with us until 2020.

The Stardust mission – a probe that caught particles from a comet's tail and returned them to Earth in 2006 – taught us far more about the very early Solar System from these fragments. Capturing these samples from comets – which formed at the centre of the Solar System but have travelled to its very edge – has helped scientists to understand more about the origin of the Solar System itself.

Deep Impact
and Rosetta

Deep Impact was a probe launched by NASA
in 2005. One part was designed to fly past the
comet Tempel 1. The second part was designed to
crash-land on the comet's nucleus! This produced
the best pictures ever taken of a nucleus. Objects
less than 10 m (33 ft) could be seen in great detail.
However, the crash-landing made such a big cloud
of dust the spacecraft flying by could not photograph the impact crater.

In 2014, ESA's spacecraft Rosetta was able
to land the module Philae on Comet 67P/
Churyumov–Gerasimenko. Sadly Philae's battery
ran out in 2 days, and because it had landed in
shadow it could not use solar energy to recharge
the battery.

Comets

- Comets are big, dirty and not-very-round snowballs that travel round the Sun. They are made up of elements created in stars that exploded a long time before our Sun was born. It is believed there are about 1 trillion of them, very far away from the Sun, waiting to come closer to us. But we can only see them when they come close enough to the Sun to have a shiny trail. We actually know of just over 6,000 comets so far.

- The largest-known comets have a central core of more than 32 km (20 miles) from one side to the other.

- When they come close to the Sun, the ice in comets turns into gas and releases the dust that was trapped inside. This dust is probably the oldest dust there is throughout the Solar System. It contains clues about our cosmic neighbourhood at the very beginning of the life of all the planets, more than 6 billion years ago.

Most of the time, comets circle round the Sun from very far away (much, much further away than the Earth). Every now and then, one of them starts to travel towards the Sun. There are then two possibilities:

1) Some, like Halley's comet, will get trapped by the Sun's gravity. These comets will then keep orbiting the Sun until they melt completely or until they hit a planet. Halley's comet's core is about 16 km (9.6 miles) long. It returns near enough to the Sun to melt down a bit and have a trail that can be seen by us about every 76 years. It was near us in 1986 and will be back in 2061. Some of the comets trapped by the Sun's gravity return near the Sun much more rarely. The Hyakutake Comet, for instance, will travel for at least 70,000 years before coming back.

2) Because they have too much speed or because they do not travel close enough to the Sun, some other comets, like Comet Swan, never come back. They pass by us once and then start an immense journey in outer space towards another star. These comets are cosmic wanderers. Their interstellar journey can take hundreds of thousands of years, sometimes less, but sometimes even more.

Light and How It Travels Through Space

One of the most important things in the Universe is the electromagnetic field. It reaches everywhere; not only does it hold atoms together, but it also makes electrons bind different atoms together or create electric currents. Our everyday world is built from very large numbers of atoms stuck together by the electromagnetic field; even living things, like human beings, rely on it to exist and to function.

Jiggling an electron creates waves in the field – this is like jiggling a finger in your bath and making ripples in the water. These waves are called electromagnetic waves, and because the field is everywhere, the waves can travel far across the Universe until stopped by other electrons that can absorb their energy. They come in many different types, but some affect the human eye, and we know these as the various colours of visible light. Other types include radio waves, microwaves, infrared, ultraviolet, X-rays and gamma rays. Electrons are jiggled all the time – by atoms that are constantly jiggling too – so there are always electromagnetic waves being produced by objects. At room temperature they are mainly infrared, but in much hotter objects the jiggling is more violent, and produces visible light. Light travels at 300,000 km (186,000 miles) per second. This is very fast, but light from the Sun still takes 8 minutes and 30 seconds to reach us; from the next nearest star it takes more than 4 years.

Electromagnetic waves move in different wavelengths. Gamma rays are short, and radio waves are long. Visible light is in the middle, between infrared and ultraviolet.

Very hot objects in space, such as stars, produce visible light, which may travel a very long way before hitting something. When you look at a star, the light from it may have been moving serenely through space for hundreds of years. It enters your eye and, by jiggling electrons in your retina, turns into electricity, which is sent along the optic nerve to your brain, and your brain says: 'I can see a star!' If the star is very far away you may need a telescope to collect enough of the light for your eye to detect, or the jiggled electrons could instead create a photograph or send a signal to a computer.

The Universe is constantly expanding, inflating like a balloon. This means that distant stars and galaxies are moving away from Earth. This stretches their light as it travels through space towards us – the further it travels, the more stretched it becomes. The stretching makes visible light look redder – which is known as the red shift. Eventually, if it travelled and red-shifted far enough, the light would no longer be visible, and would become first infrared and then microwave radiation (as used on Earth in microwave ovens). This is just what has happened to the incredibly powerful light produced by the Big Bang – after 13 billion years of travelling, it is detectable today as microwaves coming from every direction in space. This has the grand title of cosmic microwave background radiation, and is nothing less than the afterglow of the Big Bang itself.

Getting in Touch with Aliens

Dr SETH SHOSTAK

SETI (Search for Extraterrestrial Intelligence) Institute, USA

If aliens are really out there, will we ever get to meet them?

The distances between the stars are staggeringly great, so we still can't be sure that a face-to-face encounter will some day take place (assuming the aliens have faces!). But even if extraterrestrials never visit our planet or receive a visit from us, we might still get to know one another. We might still be able to talk.

One way this could happen is by radio. Unlike sound, radio waves can move through the empty spaces between the stars. And they move as fast as anything can move – at the speed of light.

Almost 50 years ago, some scientists worked out what it would take to send a signal from one star system to another. It surprised them to learn that interstellar conversation wouldn't require super-advanced technology like you often see in sciencefiction films. It's possible to send radio signals from one solar system to another with the type of radio equipment we could build today. So the scientists stood back from their chalkboards and said to themselves: if this is so easy, then no matter what aliens might be doing, they'd surely be using radio to communicate over large distances. The scientists realized that it would be a perfectly logical idea to turn some of our big antennae to the skies and see if we could pick up extraterrestrial signals. After all, finding an alien broadcast would instantly prove that there's someone out there, without the expense of sending rockets to distant star systems in the hope of discovering a populated planet.

Unfortunately, this alien eavesdropping experiment, the Search for Extraterrestrial Intelligence (SETI), has so far failed to find a single sure peep from the skies. The radio bands have been discouragingly quiet wherever we've looked, aside from the natural static caused by such objects as quasars (the churning, high-energy centres of some galaxies) or pulsars (rapidly spinning neutron stars).

Does that mean that intelligent aliens, able to build radio transmitters, don't exist? That would be an astounding discovery, because there are surely at least a hundred billion planets in our Milky Way Galaxy – and there are at least 2 trillion other galaxies! If no one is out there, we are stupendously special, and dreadfully alone.

Well, as SETI researchers will tell you, it's entirely too soon to conclude that we have no company among the stars. After all, if you're going to listen for alien radio broadcasts, not only do you have to point your antenna in the right direction, but you also need to tune to the right spot on the dial, have a sensitive-enough receiver, and be listening at the right time. SETI experiments are like looking for buried treasure without a map. So the fact that we haven't found anything so far isn't surprising. It's like digging a few holes on the beach of a South Pacific island and coming up with nothing but wet sand and crabs. You shouldn't immediately conclude that there's no treasure to be found.

Fortunately, new radio telescopes are speeding up our search for signals, and it's possible that within a few dozen years we could hear a faint broadcast from another civilization.

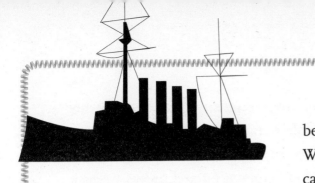

What would they be saying to us? Well, of course we can only guess, but one thing the extraterrestrials will surely know: they'd better send us a long message, because speedy conversation is simply impossible. For example, imagine that the nearest aliens are on a planet around a star that's 1,000 light years away. If we pick up a signal from them tomorrow, it will have taken 1,000 years to get to us. It will be an old message, but that's OK. After all, if you read Sophocles or Shakespeare, those are old 'messages' too, but they're still interesting.

However, if we choose to reply, our response to the aliens will take 1,000 years to get to them, and another 1,000 years will pass before their answer gets back to us! In other words, even a simple 'Hello?' and its alien response, 'Zork?', would take 20 centuries. So while talking on the radio is a lot faster than travelling in rockets for a meet-and-greet, it's still going to be a very relaxed conversation. That suggests that the aliens might send us books and books of stuff about themselves and their planet, knowing that we won't be doing a lot of chatting.

But even if they do, even if they send us *The Alien Encyclopaedia*, will we be able to read it? After all, unlike in the movies and TV, the extraterrestrials aren't going to be fluent in English or any other earthly language. It's possible that they may use pictures or even mathematics to help make their message understandable, but we won't know until and unless we pick up a signal.

No matter what they send us, detecting a radio squeal coming from a distant world would be big news. Some day soon they may tell us something extraordinarily interesting: namely, that in the vast expanses of space, humans are not the only ones watching the Universe.

And today's young people may be those who will be there to listen – and to respond. This could be you!

How Sound Travels Through Space

- On Earth there are lots of atoms close together and knocking each other around. Giving atoms a kick can make them kick their neighbouring atoms, and then those atoms kick other atoms, and so on, so the kick travels through the mass of atoms. Lots of little kicks can create a stream of vibrations travelling through a material. The air covering the Earth's surface consists of a large number of gas atoms and molecules bouncing off each other; it can carry vibrations like this, as can the sea, the rock beneath our feet and even everyday objects. The vibrations that are the right sort to stimulate our ears we call sound.

- It takes time for sound to travel through a material because an atom has to pass each kick on to its neighbours. How much time depends on how strongly the atoms affect each other, which depends on the nature of the material and other things like the temperature. In air, sound travels at around 1.6 km (1 mile) every 5 seconds. This is about 1 million times slower than the speed of light, which is why the light from a space-shuttle launch is seen almost immediately by the spectators, while the noise arrives a bit later. In the same way a lightning flash arrives before the thunder – which is the kick given to the air molecules by the sudden and intense electrical discharge. In the sea, sound travels at around five times faster than it does in air.

- In outer space it is very different. Between stars, atoms are very rare, so there is nothing to kick against. Of course, if you have air in your spacecraft, sound inside it will travel normally. A small rock hitting the outside will make the wall of the craft vibrate, and then the air inside, so you might hear that. But sounds created on a planet, or in another spacecraft, would not carry to you unless someone there converted them into radio waves (which are like light and don't need a material to carry them), and you used your radio receiver to convert them back into sound inside your ship.

- There are also natural radio waves travelling through space, produced by stars and faraway galaxies. Radio astronomers examine these in the same way that other astronomers examine visible light from space. Because radio waves are not visible, and we are used to converting them into sound using radio receivers, radio astronomy is sometimes thought of as 'listening' rather than 'looking'. But both radio and visible-light astronomers are doing the same thing: studying types of electromagnetic waves from space. There isn't really any sound from space at all.

Is There Anyone Out There?

Lord MARTIN REES

Former President of the Royal Society (2005–2010),
Trinity College, University of Cambridge

William some readers of this book walk on Mars? I hope so – indeed, I think it is very likely that they will. It will be a dangerous adventure and perhaps the most exciting exploration of all time. Throughout human history, pioneering explorers have ventured to new continents, crossed fathomless oceans, reached the North and South Poles and scaled the summits of the highest mountains. Those who travel to Mars will go in the same spirit of adventure.

It would be wonderful to traverse the mountains, canyons and craters of Mars, or perhaps even to fly over them in a balloon. But nobody would go to Mars for a comfortable life. It will be harder to live there than at the top of Everest or at the South Pole.

But the greatest hope of these pioneers would be to find something on Mars that was alive.

Here on Earth, there are literally millions of species of life – slime, moulds, mushrooms, trees, frogs, monkeys (and of course humans as well). Life survives in the most remote corners of our planet – in dark caves where sunlight has been blocked for thousands of years, on arid desert rocks, around hot springs where the water is at boiling point, deep underground and high in the atmosphere.

Our Earth teems with an extraordinary range of life forms. But there are constraints on size and shape. Big animals have fat legs but still can't jump like insects. The largest animals float in water. Far greater variety could exist on other planets. For instance, if gravity were weaker, animals could be larger and creatures our size could have legs as thin as insects'.

Everywhere you find life on Earth, you find water.

There is water on Mars and life of some kind could have emerged there. The red planet is much colder than the Earth and has a thinner atmosphere. Nobody expects green goggle-eyed Martians like those that feature in so many cartoons. If any advanced intelligent aliens existed on Mars, we would already know about them – and they might even have visited us by now!

Go to page 136 to read more about our Solar System.

Mercury and Venus are nearer the Sun than the Earth is. Both are very much hotter. Earth is the Goldilocks planet – not too hot and not too cold. If the Earth were too hot, even the most tenacious life would fry. Mars is a bit too cold but not absolutely frigid. The outer planets are colder still.

What about Jupiter, the biggest planet in our Solar System? If life had evolved on this huge planet, where the force of gravity is far stronger than on Earth, it could be very strange indeed – for instance, huge balloon-like creatures, floating in the dense atmosphere.

Jupiter has four large moons that could, perhaps, harbour life. One of these, Europa, is covered in thick ice. Beneath that there lies an ocean. Perhaps there are creatures swimming in this ocean? To search for life on Europa, NASA is considering a landing mission, but this may be difficult if Europa is covered in icy spikes, as recent research suggests it is!

But the biggest moon in the Solar System is Titan, one of Saturn's many moons. Scientists have already landed a probe on Titan's surface, revealing rivers, lakes and rocks. But the temperature is about -170°C (-274°F) where any water is frozen solid. It is not water but liquid methane that flows in these rivers and lakes – not a good place for life.

Let's now widen our gaze beyond our Solar System to other stars. There are tens of billions of these suns in our Galaxy. Even the nearest of these is so far away that, at the speed of a present-day rocket, it would take millions of years to reach it. Equally, if clever aliens existed on a planet orbiting another star, it would be difficult for them to visit us. It would be far easier to send a radio or laser signal than to traverse the mindboggling distances of interstellar space.

If there was a signal back, it might come from aliens very different from us. Indeed, it could come from machines whose creators have long ago been usurped or become extinct. And, of course, there may be aliens who exist and have big 'brains' but are so different from us that we wouldn't recognize them or be able to communicate with them. Some may not want to reveal that they exist (even if they are actually watching us!). There may be some super intelligent dolphins, happily thinking profound thoughts deep under some alien ocean, doing nothing to reveal their presence. Still other 'brains' could actually be swarms of insects, acting together like a single intelligent being. There

> Absence of evidence isn't evidence of absence.

may be a lot more out there than we could ever detect.

There are billions of planets in our Galaxy and our Galaxy itself is only one of billions. Most people would guess that the cosmos is teeming with life – but that would be no more than a guess. We still know too little about how life began, and how it evolves, to be able to say whether simple life is common. We know even less about how likely it would be for simple life to evolve in the way it did here on Earth. My bet (for what it is worth) is that simple life is indeed very common but that intelligent life is much rarer.

Indeed, there may not be any intelligent life out there at all. Earth's intricate biosphere could be unique. Perhaps we really are alone. If that's true, it's a disappointment for those who are looking for alien signals – or who even hope that some day aliens may visit us. But the failure of searches needn't depress us.

Indeed, it is perhaps a reason to be cheerful because we can then be less modest about our place in the great scheme of things. Our Earth could be the most interesting place in the cosmos.

If life is unique to the Earth, it could be seen as just a cosmic sideshow – though it needn't be. That is because evolution isn't over – indeed, it could be nearer its beginning than its end. Our Solar System is barely middle-aged – it will be 6 billion years before the Sun swells up, engulfs the inner planets and vaporizes any life that still remains on Earth. Far-future life and intelligence could be as different from us as we are from a bug. Life could spread from Earth through the entire Galaxy, evolving into a teeming complexity far beyond what we can even imagine. If so, our tiny planet – this pale-blue dot floating in space – could be the most important place in the entire cosmos.

Part Six

Time Travel . . .

Wormholes and Time Travel

Dr KIP S. THORNE

Nobel Prize-winner in Physics 2017

magine that you are an ant, and you live on the surface of an apple. The apple hangs from the ceiling by a thread so thin that you can't climb up it, so the apple's surface is your entire universe. You can't go anywhere else. Now imagine that a worm has eaten a hole through the apple, so you can walk from one side of the apple to the other by either of two routes: round the apple's surface (your universe), or by a shortcut, through the wormhole.

Could our Universe be like this apple? Could there be wormholes that link one place in our Universe to another? If so, what would such a wormhole look like to us?

The wormhole would have two mouths, one at each end. One mouth might be at Buckingham Palace in London, and the other on a beach in California. The mouths might be spherical. Looking into the London mouth (rather like looking into a crystal ball), you could see the California beach, with lapping waves and swaying palm trees. Looking into the California mouth, your friend might see you in London, with the palace and its guards behind you. Unlike a crystal ball, the mouths are not solid. You could step right into the big spherical mouth in London, and then after a brief float through a weird sort of tunnel, you would arrive on the beach in California, and you could spend the day surfing with your friend. Wouldn't it be wonderful to have such a wormhole?

The apple's interior has three dimensions (east–west, north–south and up–down), while its surface has only two. The apple's wormhole connects points on the two-dimensional surface by penetrating through the three-dimensional interior. Similarly, your wormhole connects London and California in our three-dimensional Universe by penetrating through a four-dimensional (or maybe even more-dimensional) hyperspace that is not part of our Universe.

Our Universe is governed by the laws of physics. These laws dictate what can happen in our Universe and what cannot. Do these laws permit wormholes to exist? Amazingly, the answer is yes!

Unfortunately (according to those laws) most wormholes will implode – their tunnel walls will violently collapse inwards – so quickly that nobody and nothing can travel through and survive. To prevent this implosion we must insert into the wormhole a weird form of matter: matter that has negative energy, which produces a sort of anti-gravity force that holds the wormhole open.

Can matter with negative energy exist? Amazingly, again, the answer is yes! And such matter is made daily in physics laboratories, but only in tiny amounts or only for a short moment of time. It is made by borrowing some energy from a region of space that has none, that is, by borrowing energy from 'the vacuum'. What is borrowed, however, must be returned very quickly when the lender is the vacuum, unless the amount borrowed is very tiny. How do we know? We learn this by scrutinizing the laws of physics closely, using mathematics.

Suppose you are a superb engineer, and you want to

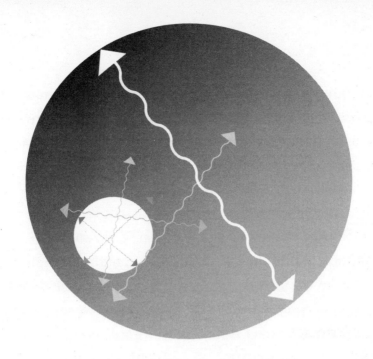

hold a wormhole open. Is it possible to assemble enough negative energy inside a wormhole and hold it there long enough to permit your friends to travel through? My best guess is 'no', but nobody on Earth knows for sure – yet. We've not been smart enough to figure it out.

If the laws do permit wormholes to be held open, might such wormholes occur naturally in our Universe? Very probably not. They would almost certainly have to be made and held open artificially, by engineers.

How far are human engineers today from being able to make wormholes and hold them open? Very, very far. Wormhole technology, if it is possible at all, may be as difficult for us as space flight was for cavemen. But for a very advanced civilization that has mastered wormhole technology, wormholes would be wonderful: the ideal means for interstellar travel!

Imagine you are an engineer in such a civilization. Put one wormhole mouth (one of the crystal-ball-like spheres) into a spaceship and carry it out into the Universe at very high speed and then back to your home planet. The laws of physics tell us that this trip could take a few days as seen and felt and measured in the spaceship, but several years as seen, felt and measured on the planet. The result is weird: if you now walk into the space-travel mouth, through the tunnel-like wormhole, and out of the stay-at-home mouth, you will go back in time by several years. The wormhole has become a machine for travelling backwards in time!

With such a machine, you could try to change history. You could go back in time, meet your younger self on a certain day, and tell yourself to stay at home because when you left for work that day, you got hit by a truck.

Stephen Hawking has conjectured that the laws of physics prevent anyone from ever making a time machine, and thereby prevent history from ever being changed. Because the word 'chronology' means 'the arrangement of events or dates in the order of their occurrence', this is called the chronology protection conjecture. We don't know for sure whether Stephen is right, but we do know two ways in which the laws of physics might prevent time machines from being made and thereby protect chronology.

Firstly, the laws might always prevent even the most advanced of engineers from collecting enough negative energy to hold a wormhole open and let us travel through it. Remarkably, Stephen has proved (using the laws of physics) that every time machine requires negative energy, so this would prevent any time machine from being made, and not just time machines that use wormholes.

The second way to prevent time machines is this: my physicist colleagues and I have shown that time machines might always destroy themselves, perhaps by a gigantic explosion, at the moment when anyone tries to turn them on. The laws of physics give strong hints that this may be so; but we don't yet understand the laws and their predictions well enough to be sure.

So the final verdict is unclear. We do not know for sure whether the laws of physics allow very advanced civilizations to construct wormholes for interstellar travel, or machines for travelling back in time. To find out for certain requires a deeper understanding of the laws than Stephen or I or other scientists have yet achieved.

That is a challenge for you – the next generation of scientists.

Space, Time and Relativity

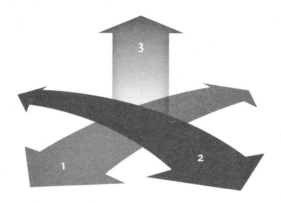

Four-dimensional Space–Time

When we want to go somewhere on Earth, usually we only think in two dimensions – how far north or south, and how far east or west. That is how maps work. We use two-dimensional directions all the time. For example, to drive anywhere you only need to go forward (or reverse), or turn left (or right). This is because the surface of the Earth is a two-dimensional space – and you only need to know the longitude and the latitude.

4

The pilot of an aeroplane, on the other hand, isn't stuck to the Earth's surface! The aeroplane can also go up and down – so, as well as its position over the Earth's surface, it can also change its altitude. When the pilot is flying the plane, 'north', 'east' or 'up' will depend on the aeroplane's position. 'Up', for example, means away from the centre of the Earth, so over Australia this would be very different from over Great Britain!

To find out about three-dimensional printing, turn to page 362.

The same is true for the commander of a spaceship far away from the Earth. The commander can choose three reference directions any way he or she wishes – but there must always be three, because the space in which we, the Earth, our Sun, the stars and all the galaxies exist is three-dimensional (longitude, latitude and altitude).

Of course, if we have something we need to get to, like a party or a sports match, it isn't enough to know where it will be held! We also need to know when. Any event in the history of the Universe therefore needs four distances, or coordinates: three of space and one of time – so, to describe the Universe and what happens within it completely, we are dealing with a four-dimensional space–time (longitude, latitude, altitude and time).

Relativity

Einstein's special theory of relativity says that the laws of nature, and in particular the speed of light, will be the same, no matter how fast one is moving. It's easy to see that two people who are moving relative to each other will not agree on the distance between two events. For example, two events that take place at the same spot in a jet aircraft will appear to an observer on the ground to be separated by the distance the jet has travelled between the events. So if these two people try to measure the speed of a pulse of light travelling from the tail of the aircraft to its nose, they will not agree on the distance the light has travelled from its emission to its reception at the nose. But because speed is distance travelled divided by the travel

Remember Einstein's theories? If not, you can read more about them on pages 7–8 and page 12.

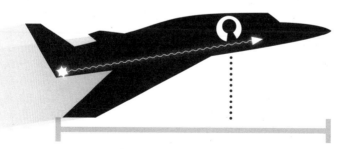

time, they will also not agree on the time interval between emission and reception – if they agree on the speed of light, as Einstein's theory says they do!

This shows that time cannot be absolute, as Newton thought: that is, one cannot assign a time to each event to which everyone will agree. Instead, each person will have their own measure of time, and the times measured by two people that are moving relative to each other will not agree.

This has been tested by flying a very accurate atomic clock round the world. When it returned, it had measured slightly less time than a similar clock that had remained at the same place on the Earth. This means you could extend your life by constantly flying round the world! However, this effect is very small (about 0.000002 seconds per circuit) and would be more than cancelled by eating all those airline meals!

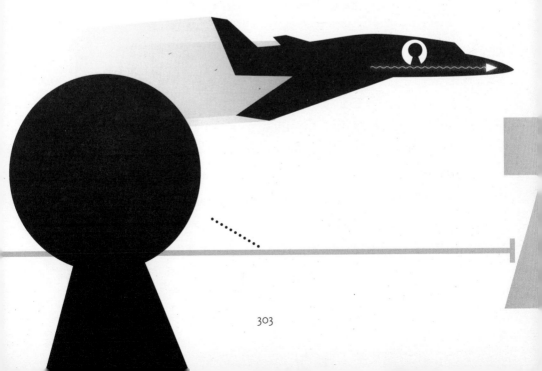

Time Travel and the Mystery of the Moving Clocks

Professor PETER McOWAN

School of Electronic Engineering and Computer Science,
Queen Mary University of London

Tick tock is the familiar sound of a clock and time passing. We all know about time – or at least we think we do! When we are together in a room, my clock shows the same time as your clock, my *tick tock* is the same as yours, and time passes at a steady beat. If you went on holiday to a distant country, your *tick tock* and mine would be the same, even if our clocks showed a different time of day. But time is an interesting thing because it can pass at different rates if you start to move very fast. When you measure the *tick tock* on a speeding spaceship, it looks slower than the *tick tock* of a clock back on Earth. Scientists call this strange effect time dilation, and it happens because light has a speed limit.

To understand time dilation we need first to understand something about light.

Light shining through the vacuum of space has a fixed speed. Scientists call this speed c, and it's around 300,000 km (186,000 miles) per second. Though light can slow down when it passes through thick stuff like glass, when it's in free space its speed is c, and that speed c happens whatever direction you shine the light in.

It's this fixed speed that gives us time dilation: time on a super-fast-moving spaceship passes more slowly than time on the Earth. This is the science behind how, in theory, someone is able to travel one way into the future – travelling so fast that only days pass, while on Earth years go by.

This all seems crazy, but that's because you can never in reality move fast enough to notice. However, if you could move at speeds near the speed of light, then your *tick tock* as seen from Earth would become more of a *tiiiiiick tooooooock*. To get a feel for why this is, we need a light clock in a see-through spaceship.

Our spaceship light clock is simple – a bulb on one side of the spaceship and a mirror on the other, with the super-powered engines at the back. When the spaceship is stationary, the bulb switches on, the light from it shoots over the distance inside the ship to the mirror and is reflected back. *Tick* is the time taken to go over to the mirror, and *tock* is the time taken to come back from the mirror.

If we had a mirror 300,000 km (186,000 miles) away, then light from a (very bright) bulb would take one second to get to the mirror and another one second to come back, because light travels at c, so that first flash is going to travel 300,000 km (186,000 miles) in one second, and take one second to come back.

Back on the stationary spaceship, our light clock will happily flash its *tick tock* at the same rate whenever we look at it, and we can use it to set all our other clocks on Earth to the same *tick tock*.

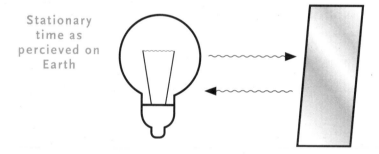

Stationary
time as
percieved on
Earth

But we now launch our see-through spaceship so that it's moving very, very quickly, and watch it from Earth. The first flash from the bulb shoots out towards the mirror but, as we look at it from being stationary on Earth, in the time the light takes to cross over to where the mirror would normally be, the mirror has moved. The distance the mirror moves will

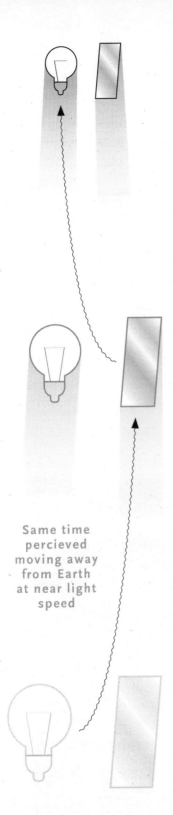

Same time
percieved
moving away
from Earth
at near light
speed

depend on how fast the spaceship is travelling; if it's very fast, then the light takes a longer sloped path to hit the mirror. Because the light travelled further and light speed c doesn't change, from our viewpoint this could only mean that the time it took to get to the shifted mirror was longer. What was *tick* on our stationary light clock now becomes *tiiick*.

On the reflection of the light, the same thing happens: the light coming from the mirror has to cover a longer distance to get back to where it started, so our *tock* is now *tooock*. This means that when we look from Earth, a moving clock runs slower than a stationary one and it seems that less time has passed on the moving spaceship. For example, when the spaceship's slow-running clock has only reached one o'clock, while it's now five o'clock on Earth, that would mean the spaceship is 4 hours into the Earth's future.

You can also think about this time dilation with some simple letter shapes. When the clock is stationary, the flashes travel back and forth like two letter I's, as the mirror and bulb are straight across from each other. The first I is the journey to the mirror, the second I is the journey from the mirror. But when our spaceship moves, the path of the light seen from the Earth is more like a V. The light now has to travel a longer distance at an angle to bounce off the shifted mirror at the bottom of the V, and again cover a longer distance to return to the start. The difference between the II and V distance means that from Earth it takes longer to have a pulse reflected back when the clock is moving, so the moving clock is slower.

That's the basic idea behind time dilation, and it's a prediction of the theory of relativity, which was one of

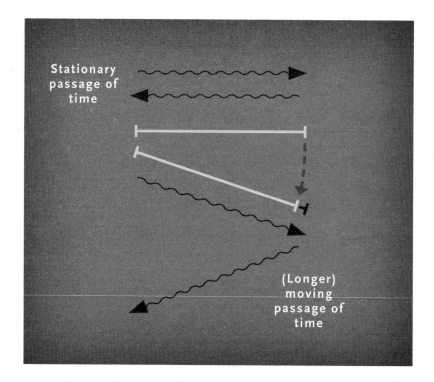

Stationary passage of time

(Longer) moving passage of time

scientist Albert Einstein's great breakthroughs (although, of course, the details of his theory are a bit more complicated). Though Earth sees my clock as running slow, if I'm on the spaceship, then from my viewpoint I'm stationary and it's the Earth that is moving away from me, so I see the Earth clock running slower, not mine. Both Earth and spaceship points of view are right, so why is it only on the spaceship that time travels into the future?

If you look closely at the mathematics, it turns out that changing speed can also cause time dilation. Since only the spaceship has to change speed and direction in order to turn round to get back to Earth, the conditions on the spaceship's flight are different from those on Earth. It's the time dilation from the spaceship's super-fast speeds and mid-course about-turn that causes the time difference that shoots the returning spaceship one way into Earth's future.

We can't yet fly spaceships at speeds anywhere near light speed, but we have some interesting experiments that show that Einstein's time-dilation idea was correct. In an accelerator – like the one at CERN in Switzerland – particles are pushed to move at speeds near the speed of light, and usefully many have their own sort of clocks on board. A particle's half-life is related to the time it takes for the particle to disintegrate into other smaller sub-particles. We can measure this half-life in the lab when the particle is stationary, and we can also measure it when the particle is moving. It turns out that when the particle moves, the 'half-life' clock does run slower than when it's stationary, and by an amount exactly predicted by Albert.

Part Seven

. . . To the Future!

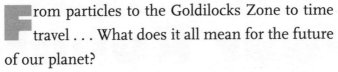

From particles to the Goldilocks Zone to time travel . . . What does it all mean for the future of our planet?

Enter the world of the unknown: in the following pages, experts from all over the globe take a unique look at what science can do for us, and how it will affect modern scientists just like you.

Our beautiful, complex, astonishing Universe is nearly 14 billion years old.

What's next?

My Robot, Your Robots

Professor PETER McOWAN

School of Electronic Engineering and Computer Science,
Queen Mary University of London

Writing about robots is as much fun as building robots. When I was younger I used to draw robots, write about robots and even build robots out of cardboard boxes and string. Now I build them for real – but I haven't forgotten that it is a lot of fun. Writers, scientists and engineers use their imaginations all the time to come up with new ways of doing things, and when it comes to robots there is no end to the possibilities; well, almost. In fact, when you have to build a robot for real you start to run into all sorts of problems, but they are always interesting problems, problems worth solving. In this chapter, I'm going to tell you some of the history of robots, some of the ways they are used today and some of the ways we might be able to use them in the future.

The dream of building a machine that looks like something real goes way back in history. One of the first built was a mechanical servant created in ancient Greece around 250 BCE; this clever device could automatically pour a cup of wine from a jug, and mix it with water as required! Its inventor, Philo of Byzantium – also known as Philo Mechanicus – came up with lots of amazing mechanical ideas, including a water-powered chirping bird, but his servant automaton was one of his most popular. An automaton (plural: automata) is the name for a mechanical device that looks like a living thing.

In the eighteenth century, automata became amazingly popular. Inventors would use the new clockwork technology of the time to create beautiful devices that looked like living dolls – dolls that could play musical instruments, perform

magic tricks and even draw pictures and write. They would tour these around the courts of Europe and make lots of money from their exhibitions; the age of the clockwork robot had arrived. In their day, they wowed the crowds, but today they look kind of creepy, alive but not quite alive, with dolls' faces, a key to wind them up and tiny mechanical bodies that jump, judder and creak.

But they set the scene for the future: for example, consider the 'Draughtsman-Writer' automaton designed by the Swiss clock-builder Henri Maillardet at the start of the nineteenth century. This was able to draw pictures and write poems.

Some early automata were what robot builders today would call programmable, as depending on the card (or brass disc, in the case of the 'Draughtsman-Writer') you placed in the automaton's slot, the machine would do different things. In essence, most robots today are similar: they have a body, they have some way of deciding how to move, a list of things to do, and a way to provide the power to do them.

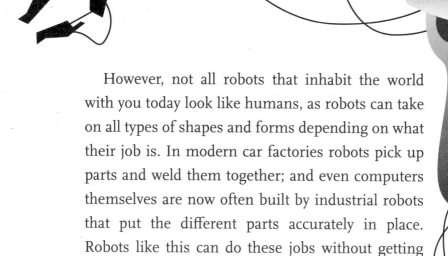

However, not all robots that inhabit the world with you today look like humans, as robots can take on all types of shapes and forms depending on what their job is. In modern car factories robots pick up parts and weld them together; and even computers themselves are now often built by industrial robots that put the different parts accurately in place. Robots like this can do these jobs without getting tired or bored, they are powered by electricity rather than clockwork, they have simple repetitive tasks to do but they get on with the job and do nothing else. They don't really need to understand their world.

On a farm, however, there can be robots that milk cows, and these robots need to be much smarter, since cows won't always be in exactly the right place at exactly the right time. These farm robots have to be able to see and make decisions. When a cow wanders in, the robot has to identify where the udders are and carefully attach the suction cups to them to remove the milk. Therefore they need to have the ability to understand a picture from a camera, and work out the best way to move their suction-cupped arms safely and gently into place. If they get it wrong, there will be trouble!

These apparently simple tasks of seeing and moving are actually really hard for machines. About half your brain (including the bit at the back of your head called the visual cortex) is right now working on understanding the world you see around you, and a great big slice in the middle of your brain – called the motor cortex – is working out how to move your muscles to do what you want your body to do.

Human brains are actually making billions and billions of calculations all the time, but what's simple to us needs to be turned into clear instructions – thousands of lines of computer code – for a robot, and as we don't yet understand exactly how the human brain does all these wonderful calculations, making a machine mimic the brain is tough. Fortunately, down on the farm, our limited understanding is enough for us to build robots with just enough intelligence to manage the job and keep the cows happy.

Ideas for robots can come from anywhere. There are scientists who study insect intelligence, for instance, since insect brains are much less complex than human brains with fewer interconnected networks of nerve cells – neurones – but insects are still smart. They have to be to survive in a difficult world – try swatting a fly! Using this example, in fact, there are robotic devices being built to fit into cars that allow cars to swerve automatically to avoid collisions; the idea for these devices came from studying flies' brains.

But what if there was an accident? Who, then, would be responsible? The car driver, the car manufacturer or perhaps even the fly? What do you think? As intelligent robots start to live in the world with us, there could be lots of questions like this.

Accepting robots into our world is complicated, and how you feel about them may also depend on where in the world you live. In the West, people tend to think of robots as sinister, out to take over the world. Often this is because that's the way robots are portrayed in films and TV. In Asia, however, robots are often presented in stories as heroic characters.

There is also something scientists call 'the uncanny valley'. If you look at how acceptable robots are, we find that robots that look like robots are generally more acceptable than robots that look like humans . . . but aren't quite the same. It's that creepy living-doll problem from the age of automata again: things just don't look right, so we don't feel happy around them.

Today's electronics and computer technologies, able to mimic the way the neurons in our brains work, as well as the movement of our limbs, allow us to build ever more lifelike robots, but they are still far from perfect. These androids – human-like robots – now buzz as the electric motors

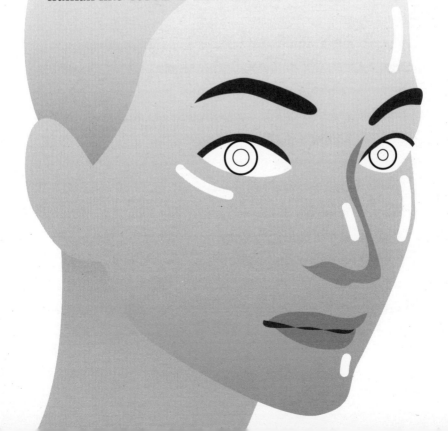

whir, rather than creak with clockwork gears, and they have complex computer programs which try to create artificially the myriad ways our brain's neurones work together, but the androids can't yet effortlessly walk up stairs, catch a ball or reliably tell the difference between silk and sandpaper. They can't unfailingly recognize faces or expressions, or single out particular voices in noisy rooms like we can; they can't yet talk, react or understand us and our world as we would naturally expect a fellow human to. They are 'not quite right', and so are hard for us to accept.

Heider and Simmel

Fritz Heider (1896–1988) was an Austrian psychologist who went to live and work in the United States in 1930. Before studying psychology, he thought of becoming an architect, then a painter, and then he studied law. None of these subjects really suited him!

Marianne Simmel (1923–2010) came from a German-Jewish family who had to flee the Nazis. They reached the United States in 1940. Aged 17, she had to work as a housekeeper while studying to get the education she needed to go to university to study psychology.

But all is not lost for today's robots; our brains hold another trick we can use. In a classic experiment by Heider and Simmel in the 1940s, people were shown random shapes moving round a screen, but when asked what was happening many came up with elaborate stories about squares falling in love with circles or larger triangles chasing smaller triangles. Our brains are smart gigantic learning machines, and one of the main ways we learn is by creating stories to make us better able to remember and understand our world. When we see robots, our brains tend to fill in the gaps that today's technologies can't yet build, so we naturally think that robots have personalities and are more intelligent than they really are, and robot-builders often give us cues to help us make these stories seem more real, and which help us to accept and use the robots better.

One big problem with robots, for instance, is the question of what powers them. When the batteries go flat, they stop, and a robot can't always be connected to the electrical mains by a cable. To get round this problem, providing power to the robot can be made part of its story. A great example is how scientists created a baby seal robot to provide comfort to residents in an old people's home and built in the need for the seal to be 'fed'. They inserted a dummy teat that was actually a recharger for the robot's batteries, so that recharging became a part of the robot's story.

In one of my projects, when the batteries in a robot dinosaur ran down it would 'go to sleep' and transfer itself to your mobile phone, where a virtual image of it could continue to play with you (while someone recharged the actual robot), then it would go to sleep on the phone and wake up in the robot body remembering what you had done with it on the phone. Can you think of a story for a robot?

How long will it be before we have robot politicians? After all, robots can make decisions based on all the facts, and they can't be corrupted, can they? When should we have robots flying our planes, driving our trains and cars, teaching in our classrooms, helping us in our homes and offices, performing surgery on us or fighting on the battle-field, making the decision to shoot by themselves? Well, we already have basic forms of these sorts of robots, but at present there is always a human somewhere in control. Should that always be the case? After all, people make mistakes all the time. Could robots do better?

New advances in nanotechnology will allow us to create microrobots that can be injected into our bodies to perform repairs or even update us, linking our bodies and minds with external technology, building a new species of humans – transhumans: robot human hybrids. Is this the stuff of nightmares or a way to improve the life of disabled people and give humanity exciting new abilities? Who knows? It might be you who builds these future robots.

I too started by reading books, having ideas and dreaming about robots. When I was about 7, I built 'Billy the robot' from boxes and string (and I still have him), then I dreamed a lot. I'm now about 50, and have been lucky enough to be involved in building robots that dance, help kids learn chess, assist the elderly in their homes and work as part of a team with people in their offices. None of my robots want to rule the world!

I have worked with loads of amazing, creative scientists and engineers to help turn my childhood robot dreams into reality. The cardboard and string have been replaced by maths, electronics and computers, but they are all proud descendants of 'Billy'.

They are my robots and I'm still having fun.

What will your robots be like?

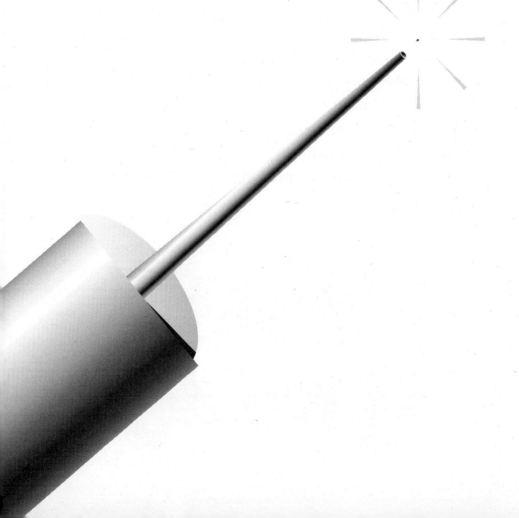

Robot Ethics

Dr KATE DARLING

Research Specialist, Massachusetts Institute of Technology

s it OK to be mean to a robot?

We all know that robots are just machines that are programmed to do things. You can't hurt their feelings and they don't experience pain like humans and animals. But . . . if verbal or physical violence towards robots still feels wrong to you, that's not crazy!

There's an interesting phenomenon in human psychology called anthropomorphism. It means that we project human qualities and emotions on to non-humans. If you've ever thought that a stuffed animal looked sad because it was thrown under the bed, or that a dog was

smiling happily at you, you've experienced anthropomor-phism. Dogs certainly have emotions, but they're harder to read than most people think! We sometimes take cues from animals and objects and imagine that they feel the same as a human would. And even though we may be wrong about what we're imagining, it's a pretty natural thing to do – evolutionarily, it's how we try to make sense of, and relate to, other beings and things.

It turns out that we anthropomorphize robots a lot. Robots combine two factors that evolution has taught us to respond to: physicality and movement. We're very physical creatures, and our brains are hardwired to see life in certain types of movements. So if we see a robot in our physical space that seems to be moving around all by itself, part of our brain thinks that the robot is doing things intentionally. And that makes it easy to imagine that the robot has goals and emotions. That's why a lot of us feel sorry for a robot when it gets stuck somewhere, even though the robot really doesn't care at all if it's stuck!

Some robots are specially designed to target this instinct. Have you seen *Star Wars*? Just like R2-D2 and the other robots in *Star Wars*, we can make real robots that use sounds and movements and other cues that we automat-ically associate with living things. A lot of children and adults enjoy playing with these robots because it's so easy to imagine that they're alive. And this imagination can even be used to help people in health and education. For example, robot animals can be pets for lonely or sick people who are

Is your robot a spy?

Maybe some day soon you'll have a robot helper at home. But before you tell your robot all your secrets, here's something to keep in mind: it's important to know a little bit about how the robot works, what purpose it serves, and what data it collects about you. For example, is the robot recording what you say? If you tell it something personal, can somebody else get that information? Most companies that sell robots probably just want you to have a cool robot, but some of them may want to collect your data to sell to other big companies. Or they may have some other idea to make more money using the robot. After all, robots are machines made by people, so they do what their creators want them to do. That's not always a bad thing. It's just a good idea to take a moment to ask: who made this robot, and why?

allergic to real animals. Teachers can use robots as friendly and engaging sidekicks to make learning more fun. Some robots are already really good at reminding people to take medicine, or comforting them, or motivating them to learn new languages. And these robots are helpful because people treat them like living things instead of like devices. It's more fun to talk to a robot than to a toaster or a computer!

In the future, robots will be in a lot of places and made for many different tasks. Some robots will be programmed to act as if they have feelings. And that brings us back to the question: is it OK to be mean to a robot? If robots don't really have feelings, it's not as bad as being mean to animals or people. But if you're nice to robots, you're not being silly. In fact, it may mean that you have a lot of empathy. Scientists like me have been researching the ways in which we treat robots like they're alive. One of our questions is whether we can learn anything about a person from how they act towards a robot. So far, we think that people who feel empathy for robots have a lot of empathy for other people too. So before being mean to a robot, consider this: if you're a kind and caring person, that may not matter to the robot, but it sure matters to you and others!

Artificial Intelligence

Dr DEMIS HASSABIS
Co-founder and CEO, DeepMind, UK

What does it mean to be intelligent? Most often in daily life, the term is used to describe how well someone does at maths, writing or another academic subject, but there is a more basic definition. At its core, intelligence means the ability to achieve goals in a wide variety of environments. Sometimes your goal might be solving a maths problem, but other times it might be something much simpler that we usually take for granted: describing the weather, playing a computer game or using a knife and fork to eat a meal. Although we don't usually think of these as particularly challenging tasks, they actually involve a tremendous amount of computer power, and it is remarkable that our brains are able to do so many different activities so well.

Intelligence is what makes humans exceptional when compared to other animals. By looking at the world around us and thinking about how it works, we have built tools, societies and civilizations to help us achieve our goals. In the span of a few tens of thousands of years – the blink of an eye relative to the history of life on Earth – humans have used our intelligence to make incredible progress: discovering electricity, building skyscrapers, curing diseases, mastering flight and even sending people to the Moon and launching probes past the limits of our Solar System. Human intellect has powered these achievements. It is unlike anything else on this planet and possibly unlike anything else in the entire Universe.

Imagine if we had intelligent machines that could help us discover even more new inventions and answer even more questions! This is exactly the goal of artificial intelligence, or 'AI'.

For a long time computers have been excellent at some tasks, such as maths and logic, but they have not been nearly as flexible as human minds. Activities that we find easy – like identifying different animals or carrying on a conversation – have generally been incredibly difficult to automate. But as computers have become faster, people have discovered new ways of programming them that have unlocked some of these abilities. Today, a number of the world's most brilliant scientists are working on designing new programs (or 'algorithms') that will enable computers, like humans, to apply intelligence to accomplish goals in a wide variety of environments. This is AI.

The most exciting area of AI research at the moment is called 'machine learning'. Machine learning takes a different approach to normal computer programming: instead of giving the computer precise step-by-step instructions, machine-learning researchers write learning algorithms that allow computers to observe the world around them and figure out answers for themselves. For instance, instead of writing a program that tells a computer that a cat has two eyes, four paws and whiskers, a machine-learning researcher might write a learning algorithm and then simply show the computer a lot of different pictures of cats. Over time, the algorithm will learn from these examples to identify cats for itself. This is very similar to how we teach human children: we might simply say, 'This is a cat', or, 'This is a dog', and let the child work out independently what the differences are between cats and dogs.

One of the most wonderful and powerful aspects of machine learning is that it is much more adaptable than regular programming. For instance, we could take the same algorithm that we used to identify cats and train the computer to identify all sorts of different animals. We could also use it to recognize faces, cars, buildings, trees and pretty much anything else. This saves us a huge amount of effort because we don't need to write specific programs for each problem! Because the algorithms are general-purpose, they can be used in all sorts of different situations.

Another benefit of learning algorithms is that, unlike normal computer programs, they can discover new facts and strategies that we did not know when we created them. For example, just recently an AI program called AlphaGo defeated the best player in the world at an ancient Chinese board game called Go. Go is sort of like chess, but much, much more complicated: it has more possible board positions than the number of atoms in the entire Universe! This makes the game very difficult, and the world's best players spend their entire lives honing their skills and trying out new tactics. AlphaGo is a machine-learning program that, like human players, learned to play the game by experimenting over time with lots of different moves and seeing which ones worked best. This meant that it discovered some novel strategies that no human player had ever used, so it not only won the game but also taught human Go players worldwide about powerful new techniques – this could never have happened with an algorithm that had been programmed conventionally with step-by-step directions. AlphaGo was a major milestone for AI because it demonstrated the power of learning algorithms to make their own discoveries in very complex domains.

Of course, we have not yet built anything nearly as flexible

or capable as the human mind; there are lots of tasks that we humans find easy but that even the best AI algorithm remains unable to do. But over the past few years machine-learning has made tremendous progress. In addition to playing Go and identifying people and animals, machine-learning programs have translated languages, improved energy efficiency and made medical advances, to list just a few of the many astounding recent examples of AI.

All this, however, is just the tip of the iceberg. Ultimately, AI scientists hope to achieve 'artificial general intelligence' (AGI) – an AI algorithm capable of doing anything the human brain can do – which would be invaluable in helping scientists conduct important research and uncover new truths. Having AGI will usher in a new age of tremendous scientific discovery: just like humans have made amazing progress over the past few thousand years by applying our own intelligence to various problems, imagine what we can accomplish if we can combine that intelligence with the power of AI! We might be able to cure most diseases, solve difficult problems like climate

Did you know the first-ever self-driving and self-sufficient cars appeared as far back as the 1980s?!

change and discover miraculous new materials that could enable everything from improved space travel to cars that drive themselves. These are ideas that once seemed fantastical but are now being proved possible every day.

This is a very exciting time for machine learning. It seems as though almost every day brings a new discovery that inches us closer to artificial general intelligence. Achieving AGI will be a huge breakthrough for mankind – something on the same level as the Moon landing or the creation of the internet. Over the course of human history we have built many tools and instruments – ranging from hammers and shovels to telescopes and microscopes – but none of them have had the same potential as AI for revolutionizing almost every aspect of human life.

Of course, nobody can say for sure how far we are from AGI. But at the speed that the field is progressing, it could happen within our lifetimes, in which case right now we are standing on the brink of a world-changing discovery, gazing into a future bursting with possibilities. There has never been a more thrilling time to be alive!

It is a fascinating and hugely exciting area to work in. In the years to come, maybe you – as one of the current generation of young people for whom computers are a familiar part of everyday life – will be one of the programmers who develop AGI further and further. You could use your skills to help our society achieve truly amazing things!

On the Ethics of AI

CARISSA VELIZ

Research Fellow, University of Oxford

with thanks to Martina Villarmea González

Ethics is the study of what is right and wrong, what we should and shouldn't do. Every person who is born finds the world in a particular state. If they lead ethical lives, when they die they will leave the world no worse than they found it. If they have been especially good, they might leave the world much better than they found it. Wouldn't it be nice to be able to say that, because you lived, the world is better than it would've otherwise been?

Imagine that, in a few years' time, you get to be a brilliant scientist; someone with the skills, knowledge and resources to invent wonderful things. Like many other scientists, you might want to create an artificial intelligence – a computer or robot that could be even smarter than you, or me, or any other human being. The first question you might want to ask if you're worried about ethics is if this scientific invention is a worthwhile project.

It's great if you find it an interesting and challenging project to spend your time on, but maybe there are projects that would do more good. Creating an AI is expensive. It takes time, effort and resources that might be put to better use on something else. Maybe you could do more good by using all your talent to invent a tool that eliminates global warming or a medicine that cures all diseases. Whether a project is worthwhile partly depends on how likely it is to be successful and how much it will cost. Perhaps the tool that eliminates global warming is quite cheap and easy to invent in comparison to an AI. Maybe it's not worth putting so much money and effort into trying to develop AI if you think that it's unlikely to work.

Suppose that, after thinking about it long and hard, you come to the conclusion that developing an AI is in fact worthwhile. You have good reason to think that it will not be too expensive; that there is a good-enough chance you will succeed in what you set out to do; and that, if you do, AI will have the power to solve global warming, diseases and many other problems.

You decide, then, to create an AI. Let's call him Alfred. How would you go about making sure that Alfred will be a force for good and not for bad? Good intentions are a good place to start. Let's say you want Alfred to be the perfect assistant. Although good intentions are important, we have all experienced a situation in which good intentions were not enough to actually do good. Sometimes we hurt people without meaning to, like when we want to offer a friend a nice cold drink and end up spilling it on her by accident.

Scientists can have good intentions and still make things that harm the world. In the novel *Frankenstein*, Mary Shelley tells the story of a scientist, Victor, who is interested in creating life. Victor is so curious and focused on his main task of making life that he forgets to think about what kind of life he might be creating. The creature that he finally brings into existence is so scary that Victor runs away from him. The monster, as he is called in the novel, finds himself abandoned by his creator, and he becomes violent and hurts people.

Frankenstein is partly a story about what can happen when scientists don't take ethics into account. So, how do you make sure that Alfred does not become like Frankenstein's monster? First, you want to design Alfred with the right values in mind. You want him to be not only super smart, but also super kind, funny and helpful. To that end, you make your best effort to bake in the right ingredients so that he turns out to be a decent guy. Then you might want to check whether Alfred actually does what you designed him to do. Before you set Alfred loose in the world, then, you might want to test him out in a lab. For example, you might put him in situations in which people need help and see whether Alfred really is as kind and helpful as you want him to be. If it turns out he is grumpier than you expected, you might have to go back into the lab and tweak him until you get it right.

Let's suppose you finally manage to get Alfred to be kind, funny and helpful. Now your job is to make sure that he will continue to be a good guy. To that end, you should ask yourself: what can go wrong? Let your imagination run wild. For instance, suppose you ask Alfred to do something extremely urgent and important, something that will save lives, and he runs out of battery in the middle of the task. That could be a disaster, and it would make him (unintentionally) unhelpful. So you have to make sure that can't happen, maybe by designing a way for Alfred to generate his own energy every time he moves, so that he does not depend on batteries.

Something else to consider is that some tools can be used for both good and evil. Gunpowder, for example, was invented in China as a medicine. Only later was it used differently, first for fireworks, and then for firearms. Sometimes it is useful to think like a villain in order to avoid harm. Imagine you are the most evil villain. How might you use Alfred for bad? Perhaps you might hack into his central system and make him act like Frankenstein's monster. To avoid such a possibility, you might want to make sure Alfred has such a secure system that hacking him is almost impossible. You might also want to design a remote off switch, so you can retain the power to turn Alfred off in case something goes wrong.

Throughout the history of science, some scientists have come to regret what they invented. Mikhail Kalashnikov, for instance, invented an automatic rifle that would help soldiers defend his country. When that rifle was later sold across the world and used to hurt innocent people in countless conflicts, he felt responsible for those harms, and he wished he hadn't invented his rifle. One of the dangers of science is that you can't uninvent what you have invented. In Kalashnikov's case, it was easy to foresee how his invention would be used to cause harm. Better to be like those many other scientists who can be proud of what they invented, like Edward Jenner, who saved millions of lives by developing the world's first vaccine.

When you grow up, if you take ethics into account from the start, if you make things that will be used for good, and if you make every effort to avoid unintended bad consequences, your inventions could make people happier, healthier and wiser. And what better way to spend your time and energy than trying to make the world a better place?

Kalashnikov's Dilemma

Mikhail Kalashnikov, a soldier and engineer, invented his rifle just after the Second World War for the army of the Soviet Union to use. It was a very simple design, straightforward to operate, and it could be easily maintained even in the most difficult conditions. People all over the world used it – or illegal copies of it. A few months before Kalashnikov died, he wrote a letter to a Russian clergyman and asked: 'I keep having the same unsolved question: if my rifle claimed people's lives, then can it be that I . . . a Christian and an Orthodox believer, was to blame for their deaths?'

What do you think?

What Is a Computer?

Mathematical Laws

It is a marvellous feature of the Universe that everything in it seems to follow mathematical laws – anything from a planet to a beam of light to a sound wave – so we can predict what it can do by performing mathematics.

A computing machine turns this round – we design and assemble a collection of parts that will behave according to some mathematics of our choosing. We allow the machine to then behave naturally (to 'run') and it performs the mathematics and gives us an answer. If the theory behind the machine, the way it is built and our measurements are all sufficiently accurate, we can trust the final answer to be accurate.

Nowadays, we are used to the idea that a computer can be programmed to do almost anything if it has enough memory and processing power, and that the programs themselves are just more data. But the computer you use today is a long way from the earliest designs . . .

A Very Early Analogue Computer

Way back in the second century BCE in Greece, a very early computing machine – the Antikythera mechanism – was built to simulate the cyclic behaviour of the Sun, Moon and planets using rotating gear wheels. The designer of the machine drew an analogy between the celestial objects moving around in the sky and bronze wheels, carefully arranged through a complex mechanism so that they would accurately reflect the arrangement in the sky of those celestial bodies at different times. Since it is based upon an analogy with a specific physical system, it is an example of an analogue computer.

A slide rule – a ruler with a sliding central strip – is also an example of an early analogue computer. This handheld device was invented in the seventeenth century and widely used until the arrival of pocket-sized electronic calculators in the 1970s. It is based upon the mathematics of logarithms.

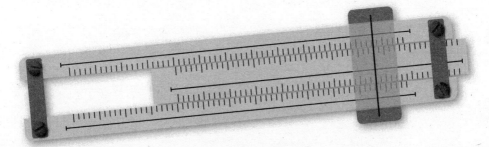

Antikythera Mechanism

In 1900, sponge divers working off the island of Antikythera in the Mediterranean Sea found an ancient shipwreck. Then, in 1901, they brought to the surface a corroded lump of metal, which had once been housed in a wooden box. Over the years, using the latest technologies, scientists found it was made of bronze and had over 30 gears (the biggest had 223 teeth). On other pieces of the machine there were inscriptions. As well as predicting astronomical positions, the mechanism could foretell eclipses and the 4-year cycle of games like the Olympics. The ability to make something as complicated as this had been lost for centuries.

But analogue computers have clear limits. The main disadvantage is that, once created, an analogue computer can only solve one type of problem with a fixed accuracy. A different problem may require different mathematical behaviour, and so need a different analogy, a different design and a different machine.

A human being, on the other hand, approaches calculation differently. They might start by writing down a set of equations, then transform these equations into other equations step by step using the rules of mathematics – a familiar process that you will know from school, e.g. solving quadratic equations.

A new form of computational device was needed to tackle problems in this way.

A Computer Powered by Steam!

Mechanical calculators followed – Blaise Pascal's of the seventeenth century was groundbreaking at the time. Then, in 1837, Charles Babbage designed an Analytical Engine which (if it had been built) would have been the first programmable computer – it would have used punched cards for programs and data, used only mechanical parts, and been capable of performing like a universal Turing machine – although it would also have been 100 million times slower than a modern computer! And it was powered by steam . . .

There's more about the Turing machine on page 350.

Blaise Pascal
(1623—1662)

Blaise Pascal was a French child prodigy. He was a mathematician, physicist, inventor and theologian. Aged 16, he wrote a paper on geometry that was so impressive that some thought it had to be his father's work.

In 1638, Pascal's father was sent to the city of Rouen to try to sort out its taxes which were in a dreadful mess. Seeing how hard his father was working to bring order to the chaos, Pascal, then 18, invented a mechanical calculator that could add and subtract. In later years, he refined the machine several times, but it was never a commercial success. However, it made him a pioneer in what would eventually become computer engineering.

Pascal was also responsible for the first bus service in Paris!

Charles Babbage
(1791–1871)

Charles Babbage was a British mathematician, inventor
and computer pioneer. He became a Fellow of the Royal
Society when he was 24, and he co-founded the Analytical
Society, the Astronomical Society and the Statistical
Society. Babbage held the Lucasian Chair of Mathematics
at Cambridge University, but never gave a lecture. He
devised two machines for making mathematical calculations, the Difference Engine in 1823 and the Analytical
Engine in 1837, which could be instructed by punched
cards. These machines could also store information in
a memory, and had a mill – a calculating unit – and a
printer, features identical to a modern computer. Sadly,
Babbage couldn't raise the money to fund them or find
the engineering expertise to make the parts. In the late
twentieth century the Science Museum in London used
Babbage's designs to make scaled-down versions of the
machines and they worked.

Ada Lovelace, who worked with Babbage, wrote the
first algorithm (or computer program) and was the first to
recognise it could be used for more than pure calculation.

From Turing to the First Digital Computers

A digital computer is a machine designed to follow algorithms automatically (like a human being might follow an algorithm, only much faster). In practice, it turns an input whole number (possibly very big) into an output whole number.

Why Whole Numbers?

It is easy to turn text into numbers – for example, in the ASCII scheme, 'A' is represented by 65 and 'Z' by 122. For actual numbers, in practice we always want to deal with fractions to a certain number of decimal places (or precision), e.g. 99.483. This is the same as 0.99483 times 100 (or 10 x 10, written mathematically as 10^2). So a digital computer only really has to store the whole numbers (integers) 99483 and the number 2, which tells us the power of 10 that is used (10^2). A real computer more normally works with binary digits (bits) which take the values 0 or 1 only, and any data – numbers, text, images, program instructions – can be represented (coded) by integers in binary notation, and put together as one long binary number in the computer's memory.

In 1949, Cambridge University built and started to use a valve-based, electronic and Turing-complete computer, EDSAC, for research, and over the following decades the electronics shrank, first from tubes to transistors, then to integrated circuits and microprocessors with very large numbers of electronic parts etched on to single pieces of silicon.

Computers Today

A computer today is a machine we expect to be able to read and store digital data and instructions, and then automatically do what we want it to do at the press of a few keys – or by moving a mouse, or by swiping, pinching or touching a screen. It is a lot smaller than its predecessors too. And as the electronics shrank, with more and more tiny parts crammed closer and closer together, the speed of a computer increased enormously.

But, unlike the Turing machine way back in the 1930s, a real computer still only has a finite amount of memory – it might, for example, have 2 GB of RAM (random access memory). It also has to perform basic operations at a very high speed – maybe 20,000,000,000 steps or 'floating point operations' per second (20 gflop/s).

For example, when you double-click on an image file on your laptop, the viewer application and the image file are both read into memory from the disk, then the processor runs the application instructions on the image data to decode it into the correct coloured dots to send to the screen so you can see what you asked for. And see it quickly too.

A typical computer today also has permanent storage

(a hard disk) which lets you turn the computer off without losing your files. It often has a connection to other computers and most likely is able to log on to the internet.

Many homes now have a personal computer – or more than one – and individual people can even carry one in a pocket on a tablet, or access the internet on a smartphone. New technology is coming out every year, and the computers of the future may look very different.

- One byte is a group of 8 bits, which is enough to store any letter of the alphabet.

- One gigabyte is 1,073,741,824 bytes.

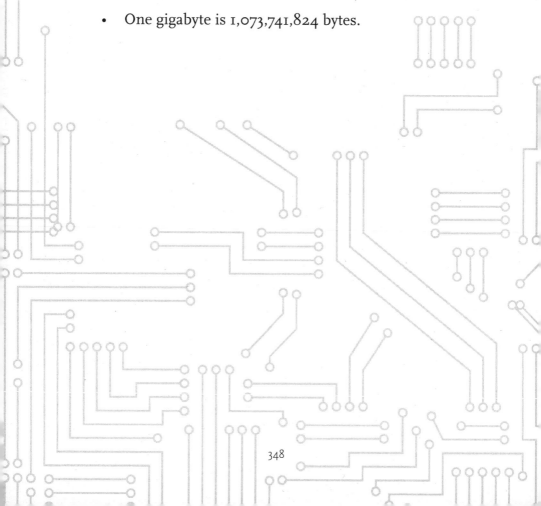

Alan Turing
(1912—1954)

Alan Turing was a mathematician, computer scientist and codebreaker who is most famous for his extremely important role in defeating the Nazis in the Second World War. During his life, he was perse-cuted for being a gay man. In 2009, the British Prime Minister Gordon Brown issued a public apology for the appalling way Turing was treated while he was alive. A 2017 law retrospectively pardoned men who were imprisoned for their sexuality, and it's affection-ately known as the Alan Turing law.

Alan showed a talent for maths and science very early on, and later in life he created the Turing machine, an imaginary computer that could theoreti-cally calculate absolutely anything.

His codebreaking skills came into play when he created a computer that decoded secret messages enemy soldiers were sending to each other – people say now that his invention saved over 14 million lives in the Second World War!

The Universal Turing Machine

An Imaginary Device

n 1936, a 'computer' was a human being performing calculations. The Turing machine developed by genius mathematician Alan Turing was intended to be a simple imaginary device capable of reproducing everything a human computer might need to do while calculating. The machine is therefore a mathematical, rather than a real-world, device to be used to understand what computation is, and what can be achieved by computation. But it could not exist in reality; for example, it is assumed to have both infinite 'memory' and an unlimited time in which to operate, neither of which are feasible.

A String of 0s . . .

The operation of a machine is first defined by a finite list of coded instructions. Imagine a very long tape on which is written a very long string of 0s (as long as the tape itself). The tape stretches out forever in both directions (assume it is infinitely long) and represents the 'memory' of the computing machine. Sprinkled among these 0s are finitely many 1s which represent the 'data' given to the machine. Sitting on this tape is the processing device (the processor) that can read just the one symbol that is currently directly beneath it and it can leave it as it is, or replace it with either 0 or 1.

It also has a clock which ticks steadily, and at each tick of the clock, the processor reads the symbol it can currently see. It then does one of two things depending on what it just read and its current state. It can:

- change the symbol beneath, marking it as 0 or 1, then move one position either left or right along the tape, maybe change to a different state, and wait for the next tick;

- or do the same but then halt (turn off).

What it actually does depends on the rules (the 'program') we give it, and what it finds on the tape. As an example, let's assume that the machine starts out in state o, with a long string of os on the tape, and that somewhere to the right of it some of the os have been replaced by 1s – these 1s form a pattern which is the binary number we give the machine as its input.

Then a good rule to start with is: *if in state o and we read o, then switch to state o, write o and move right.*

This means that when the machine sees o initially (when it is in state o), it stays in state o, does not change the o on the tape and moves one step right. If the tape one step right still says o, the same happens – the machine stays in state o, leaves the tape as it found it and marches another step right.

This happens at each tick of the clock, until the machine finally reaches the first of the 1s written on the tape. It now needs a rule which tells it what to do when it reads a 1 in state o. The simplest rule would be to: *stay in state o, write 1 and move another step right and halt.* The 1 will now appear on the left of the machine, and is the result of the computation.

We could describe this very simple computation as *v*, where by valid we mean 'contains at least one 1'. If there were no 1s written to the right of the machine when it starts, it would simply carry on marching right looking for a 1 forever – it would not halt but carry on working fruitlessly! This can happen on a real computer – a program can endlessly 'loop' or 'spin' until the entire computer crashes.

This possibility is unfortunately a fundamental property

both of Turing machines and real computers. However, we can stop this happening straight away by insisting that 'valid' inputs contain at least one 1, so that this first rule cannot simply be used forever.

Every Possible Calculation

Given enough time and the ability to write as many 1s on the tape as required, every mechanical operation with whole numbers that we can think of could be performed by feeding a Turing machine with the input number on the right of the machine, starting the clock and waiting for it to halt, then reading the answer on the left of the machine. It includes every arithmetic calculation a human with pen and paper could ever do, and Alan Turing proposed that what his Turing machine can compute should be taken as a definition of what can be computed at all. Amazingly, nearly 80 years after his theories, this is still widely believed to be a good definition because every known design for a digital computing machine can only compute what a Turing machine could compute.

Turing also showed mathematically that even a Turing machine cannot solve every problem! Put another way, some problems in mathematics are uncomputable – mathematicians can't be replaced by computers yet.

What Can't a Computer Do?

All known computer designs (including quantum computer designs) can compute no more than a Turing machine could compute if given enough time and memory. However, Turing was able to prove that some problems in mathematics are uncomputable, that is to say, they cannot be solved by a Turing machine – and hence not by any known computer today! He demonstrated this with a problem concerning Turing machines themselves, known as the halting problem.

The Halting Problem

When will a Turing machine halt? If it only has one state (state 0), then only two rules are needed – what to do if the machine reads 0 or 1. There are varied ways these rules could lead to different results, depending on how the 1 rule is formulated:

- The 0 rule says leave 0 and march right, continuing until it finds the input of a number 1, then halt. The machine halts and outputs the answer.
- But a Turing machine could find itself in an endless loop: choosing 'if 1 is read, write 1 and move left' would make the machine move back to the previous 0, then move back to the 1 at the next tick of the clock (following the 0 rule), and then repeat these two moves forever.
- It is also easy to make a Turing machine that will not ever halt. Changing the 1 rule to 'if 1 is read, write 0 and move left' will cause the machine to move back to the previous 0, then return, but this time it sees 0 and continues past until the next 1. The machine will turn all the 1s into 0s and then disappear off to the right forever.

Machine 'H'

Alan Turing himself posed the question: is there an algorithm that, when fed with the program of any Turing machine and some extra input, will output the answer 0 if that machine with that input doesn't ever halt and output an answer?

Suppose for the moment that such an algorithm existed – then there would be a Turing machine to perform it. Furthermore, there would be a machine that could test whether any Turing machine would not halt when the input was its own program. Let's call this machine H and input data such that H halts if, and only if, its input is the program of a Turing machine which doesn't halt when input with its own program.

So what happens if we feed H with its own program?

If it does halt, then it is an example of a Turing machine which halts when input with its own program – but then H was designed not to halt when fed with the program of such a machine!

If it doesn't halt, then H is a machine which doesn't halt when input with its own program, but that means that H fed with the H program should halt, because it was designed specifically to detect such machines.

Either way, this is a contradiction! A nonsensical situation like this tells a mathematician that what they were assuming is true was wrong. Constructing the imaginary Turing machine H – which cannot exist – was therefore very clever. It proved there cannot be a Turing machine able to compute whether any Turing machine with any input doesn't halt. And if this question cannot be settled by a Turing machine, therefore it is uncomputable on any computer we can currently imagine building.

Put simply, a computer can't solve this problem!

Infinite Numbers

The number of possible programs and Turing machines is infinite, but because every computer program can be turned into one big binary number a mathematician would describe the set of all programs or machines as countably infinite, because we can list them in order of size.

But there are much bigger infinities, for example the

infinity of decimals with infinite decimal places – these are called the 'real numbers'. There are real numbers whose digits cannot be generated by a computer.

For example, the real number pi (which you use in working out the circumference of a circle, for instance, and you probably know stands for 3.142) can be written out to any number of decimal places by a computer. The first few are 3.1415926535 and a computer has done this to trillions of decimal places. Most real numbers, though, cannot be generated like this: they are fundamentally uncomputable – a computer can't do it!

The Future?

Some theorists speculate that new types of computer, relying on as yet unknown physics, will be discovered in the future that can compute more than a Turing machine can compute, and that the human brain (the original 'computer') may even turn out to be one of these.

There is no general agreement on whether the human brain could be described by a sufficiently complicated Turing machine.

Quantum Computers

Dr RAYMOND LAFLAMME

Former Director of the Institute of Quantum Computing,
University of Waterloo, Canada

Computers have become integral to almost all aspects of our daily lives. Today's computers are in our homes and our cars, and most of us carry one with us everywhere we go in our mobile devices. This technological revolution was made possible by our understanding and harnessing the properties of the world around us. At the heart of that understanding is mathematics.

A Challenge for Mathematicians

In 1900, a German mathematician – David Hilbert – posed a list of 23 problems for mathematicians to solve. When British mathematician Alan Turing worked on one of the problems, which asked mathematicians to find out if we could always discover if a mathematical proposition was true in a finite amount of time, he tackled it by proposing to build a hypothetical machine that would derive theorems in a mechanical way, the Turing machine. It was a blueprint for today's classical computers.

Classical Versus Quantum

Scientists like Galileo, Newton, Maxwell and others described the world around us to a high degree of accuracy, coming up with the theories of classical mechanics. But when scientists began working at the scale of atoms and molecules, classical approaches broke down and they needed a new set of theories and rules: quantum mechanics.

These rules are very different from those of classical mechanics. For instance, the superposition principle states that if A is a solution of an equation of quantum mechanics and B is also a solution, then A+B is also a solution. What does that mean? In the case of an electron, it means that if we have one solution with an electron here, and another solution with an electron there, we can have a solution with

Read about Schrödinger on page 104.

a single electron being here and there at the same time. Pushing this possibility to its limits led the physicist Schrödinger to show that at the quantum level we could see a cat alive and dead at the same time – something we certainly don't see at our scale!

Using Quantum Principles with Computers

1. First we transform a bit of information into a quantum bit, or qubit for short – and this can be encoded in the superposition of the state 0 and 1 at the same time!

2. If we have two qubits, they can therefore be in the superposition of four states: 00, 01, 10 and 11. Now imagine three qubits: 000, 001 . . . 111: a total of eight states.

3. You can see that the number of states grows exponentially with the number of qubits. Just by changing the classical *or* (0 or 1) to a quantum *and* (0 and 1), we can have an exponential increase in our computing power!

4. This means that if we change the rules with which we compute, we can develop new algorithms and drastically change the type of problems we can solve too, though quantum computers would not necessarily have an advantage on all problems.

5. For some problems, quantum computers therefore are formidable devices. An example of a quantum algorithm is factoring large numbers which are the product of two primes – a hard problem for classical computers and

the basis of most of today's cybersecurity. A quantum computer would be able to solve factoring problems with ease and break encryptions. Quantum algorithms will also be applicable in other complex disciplines such as materials science (where we want to create new quantum materials and understand their performance), chemistry (to predict the behaviour of large atoms and molecules and apply it to drug design, for example), health care (by constructing new types of sensors) and much more that we have not yet imagined. These principles have allowed us to develop a new language, which is the proper one for talking and listening to quantum particles such as atoms and molecules.

Quantum mechanics has provided a key to understanding the very building blocks of our world. Quantum information science gives us an incredible opportunity to harness the power of quantum mechanics for the development of mind-boggling technologies such as the quantum computer, quantum cryptography, quantum sensors and more that have not even been imagined today.

3D Printing

Dr TIM PRESTIDGE
Divisional CEO, Halma PLC

What is 3D printing, how is it different to 2D printing, and why is it so exciting?

What does '3D' mean?

The 'D' stands for 'dimensional', so something that is 3D, three-dimensional, is something that has the following dimensions:
- a length (one)
- a width (two)
- a height (three)

So, while a picture on a piece of paper is a two-dimensional image (flat on the paper), physical objects that you interact with every day (like your bike, your dinner and your nose) are all 'three-dimensional'.

Slicing a Sausage!

2D printing (two-dimensional) is what we usually think of when we say 'printing' – for example, using a printer connected to a computer at home or in your school or library.

A 2D printer usually:

- uses special inks to make the 2D images on paper.
- takes an electronic file that describes a whole 2D image – like a photograph from a digital camera or a document from a word processor – and then electronically 'slices' it up into lots of very thin strips. This process is sometimes called salami-slicing because it's a bit like a chef chopping a salami sausage into slices!
- takes each electronic slice in turn and carefully squirts coloured inks on to a matching section of paper to produce a precise image of that slice.
- then moves down and does the same for the next slice, and then the next, until finally the entire image has been built up on the paper one slice at a time.
- Artists and filmmakers can make 2D objects appear 3D by using tricks: like perspective in pictures and 3D special effects in movies. But these are optical illusions and the images themselves are 2D as they only have a width (one) and a height (two).

Magic Machines

When my son was younger, he would watch with fascination as our printer whirred away producing photographs and letters. He'd also watch carefully if we bought something (like a toy) on the internet – he would wait expectantly by the printer for whatever we'd just bought to plop out of it! I guess that would make complete sense to a 4-year-old. The funny thing is, for some types of toys, this is now close to reality.

Making a Real 3D Object

In 3D printing, what is made is not just a 2D image but a real 3D object. The machines that do this are called 3D printers or additive manufacturing machines.

- It begins, like 2D printing, with an electronic file. However, this is now a special type of electronic file called a CAD model (CAD stands for computer-aided design) which describes every single detail about the object to be 3D-printed.

    If you look at the CAD model of an object on a computer screen, you can see an image of what the object looks like from the outside, but you can also 'fly through' to see what the object looks like from any point inside it.

- The 3D printer salami-slices the CAD model into electronic slices, one on top of another, where each slice might be about 20 microns thick.

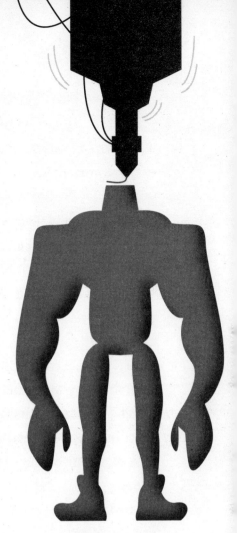

- Although all of the slices are 3D because they have thickness (or length) as well as width and height, the 3D printer treats each slice as a 2D cross-section showing precisely what the object would look like if it were carefully cut through.

- The 3D printer prints out each slice – starting with the lowest – just like a printer would a 2D image. But instead of squirting ink on to paper, it produces all the details in each slice as a 20-microns-thick layer of 'stuff' (which can be liquid plastic, wax or metals, like silver, titanium or steel).

- The material for one slice dries and hardens, then the 3D printer indexes (moves up) and produces the next slice as another 20-microns-thick layer on top of the previous one.

- This process is repeated over and over until all the slices of the CAD model have been printed one on top of another to produce a real 3D object!

20 microns – or 1/50th of a millimetre – is approximately 25% of the thickness of one of the hairs on your head! A CAD model of an object which is 10 cm high would therefore be salami-sliced into about 5,000 electronic slices!

Facts about 3D Printers

- The most common material used is plastic, as it can be easily squirted out in very small amounts as a liquid and will quickly harden into a solid. It is also ideal for making prototypes (models of new things like buildings or cars). As modern machines can use several different kinds of plastic at the same time and can print in colour, prototypes can be very realistic. This is still the biggest application for 3D printers.

- There are two common types of 3D printers used today.

  Extrusion Machines: the material is forced through a nozzle, rather like using a piping bag to ice a cake. These machines are especially good when using more than one type of colour or material, since more nozzles can easily be added.

  Bed Machines: these are most commonly used with powdered metals. Enough powder is poured out to fill one slice completely, then a power laser fuses (melts and joins) the powdered metal into a solid shape at precisely the right places in the slice. Once the model is complete, the excess powdered metal is brushed away.

- Over the next few years scientists expect that machines using plastic could become more common in peoples' homes, allowing you to download patterns and 3D-print things like made-to-measure bike helmets or personalized tools.

- 3D printers in factories use materials like metals and ceramics, for example to print out parts for jet aeroplanes that are lighter and stronger, thereby making the aeroplanes safer and more fuel-efficient.

- Medical devices like implants for new hips and teeth, and cranial plates (used to repair holes in skulls) can also be 3D-printed, because this process allows them to be made specifically for the person they will be fitted into.

Robots of the Future?

Today's 3D printers are still quite slow and can only make things out of a few different materials at the same time – it would not yet be possible to print a complete robot since you would need complicated interlocking parts made of many materials: metal parts, gears and motors, magnets, wires, plastics, oil, grease, silicon, gold – even rare things like yttrium and tungsten!

But 3D printers could easily make parts for robots within a fully automated factory. The parts could then be unloaded from the 3D printers by unloading robots, polished by polishing robots, and then assembled by assembly robots . . .

Robots using 3D printers (with other technology too) to make robots? Is this something you will see in the future?

Driverless Cars

Driverless cars – sounds like science fiction!

Driverless cars already exist! Also known as robotic or self-driving cars, these are vehicles that can perform the main functions of a normal car without a human being in charge. They can sense the environment around them, using radar, computer systems and GPS, so they can navigate as well as get round obstacles or deal with changing conditions on the roads.

For instance, the Google self-driving car – powered by software called Google Chauffeur – has been running for a number of years already and their latest car has no steering wheel or pedals!

Driverless cars could be really useful. They do long journeys without getting tired, and they could help disabled or blind people who can't drive ordinary cars to get around. Cars driven by robots, if they function properly, might be

safer than cars driven by humans: robots don't look out of the window or fiddle around changing the radio station, answer a mobile phone or have arguments with passengers! But all machines can malfunction – and getting rid of human error doesn't mean there won't be accidents. If a driverless car malfunctions while in motion, it's possible that the passengers in the car wouldn't be able to control the vehicle. And what would happen if we all forgot how to drive? Would that be a good idea? What would happen to all the bus, coach and taxi drivers? What jobs would they do if robots took over the road?

Some countries in Europe are already drawing up plans to create transport networks for driverless cars, and thinking how laws might need to be changed to cover their use. Keep your eyes peeled – you might see a driverless car near you soon.

Problems Facing Our Planet

Asteroid Attack!

An asteroid is a rocky fragment left over from the formation of the Solar System about 4.6 billion years ago. Scientists estimate there are probably millions of asteroids in our Solar System.

Asteroids typically range in size from as little as a metre, or 2 feet, to hundreds of miles, or kilometres, across.

Once in a while, an asteroid will get nudged out of its orbit – for example by the gravity of nearby planets – possibly sending it on a collision course with the Earth.

Around once a year, a rock the size of a family car crashes into the Earth's atmosphere but burns up before it reaches the surface.

Once every few thousand years, a chunk of rock about the size of a playing field hits the Earth, and every few million years, Earth suffers an impact from a space object – an

asteroid or a comet – large enough to threaten civilization.

If an asteroid or a comet – a rocky ice ball that slingshots round the Sun – were to hit the surface of the Earth, it is possible that it could crash through the surface, releasing a flood of volcanic eruptions. Nothing would survive the impact.

An asteroid smashed into the Earth 65 million years ago. This could be what wiped out the dinosaurs – the impact sending up a cloud of fine dust, blocking out the sunlight and dooming the dinosaurs and many other species to extinction.

A meteoroid is a chunk of rock that flies through our Solar System; a meteorite is what you call that piece of rock if it lands on the Earth.

Gamma Ray Burst . . . Game Over!

We also face the exotic threat of extinction by gamma rays from space.

When very massive stars reach the ends of their lives and explode, they not only send hot dust and gas across the cosmos in an expanding cloud. They also shoot out deadly beams of gamma rays, like lighthouse beams. If the Earth were directly in the path of such a beam, and if the GRB (gamma ray burst) happened close enough to us, the beam could rip our atmosphere apart, causing clouds of brown nitrogen to fill the skies.

Such explosions are rare. One would need to happen within a few thousand light years of our planet to do real damage, and the beam would need to hit us very precisely. Thus, astronomers who have studied the problem in detail are not that worried!

Self-Destruct!

We've already done a lot of damage to our planet, without any help from asteroids or gamma rays.

The Earth is suffering from overpopulation.

All those extra people mean we will need to grow more food, putting a greater strain on the Earth's natural resources and sending even more gases into the Earth's atmosphere. There's been a lot of argument about climate change. But scientists are clear that the planet is getting warmer and that human activity is the reason for this change. They expect this change to continue, meaning that the world will get hotter and some areas will experience heavy rainfall while others suffer from drought. Sea levels are expected to rise, which could make life very difficult for people who live on coastlines.

There are more and more humans on Earth but fewer and fewer other species. Extinction of other animals is a growing problem, and we are seeing whole groups of species disappear from the face of the Earth. It seems a real pity that we are destroying our beautiful and unique planet just as we are learning how it really works.

Globally, nearly a quarter of all mammal species and a third of amphibians are threatened with extinction.

The Earth is home to over 7 billion people.

The Future of Food

Dr MARCO SPRINGMANN

Senior Researcher in Population Health,
Oxford Martin School

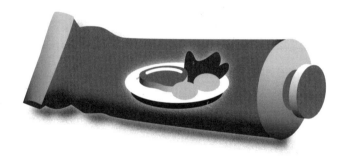

Many predictions have been made about the future of food. They range from 'edible air' to 'meals in a pill'. Highly engineered novelty food products have been the staple of food futurists, and indeed of early space missions. Had you been on board a spaceship in the 1960s, you would have had toothpaste-type tubes, with liquefied or puréed food for breakfast, some bite-sized food cubes for lunch, and maybe some freeze-dried food powders for supper. Not the most appetizing prospect!

But the nutritionists' early enthusiasm for vitamin pills and 'meals in a pill' has now given way to a renewed focus on wholefoods. Take the humble apple, for example: apples, like other fruits and vegetables, contain a complex mixture of thousands of compounds that protect cells from damage. When eaten in the form of the whole fruit, apples can help prevent us from developing chronic diseases such as cancer and heart disease.

Scientists have tried to extract what they thought of as the active ingredients – for example, vitamin C from fruit such as apples, vitamin E from green leafy vegetables such as spinach, and beta-carotene from orange vegetables such as carrots. However, it has been found that eating those extracts in pill form does not have any preventive health effects in most cases, and it could even sometimes lead to an increase in chronic disease. You do have to eat the whole food to get all the health benefits.

What you would now find in the canteen of a spaceship, or on board a space station, would resemble more what you can find in one down on Earth. How about some mashed potatoes, nuts, broccoli and even an apple a day?

Let's get back to thinking a bit more about the future of food. For that purpose, it might be instructive to consider what influences what we eat, and how what we eat influences our health and our planet (and any future planets we might find).

I'll start with what might seem like a simple question: why do you eat what you eat?

Maybe you eat a specific meal because you like its taste, or you are hungry. Maybe you eat it because it is there, and somebody has prepared it for you. Why do you think that person chose to cook that meal and not something else? Why is that specific meal there to begin with?

Scientists consider a similar set of questions when trying to predict how and what the world might eat in the future. They start with what can and has been produced in the past, and where. In the UK, that would currently include milk, meat, wheat and root vegetables such as potatoes and carrots; and of course also some fruit, like apples and strawberries. Then they look at how many people are around to eat the food produced, how much money those people have to spend on their food, what other foods might be available somewhere else, and how easy it would be to exchange some foods that are closer for foods that are further away.

What the scientists observed was: as people become richer, they consume more in general, and in particular more meat, dairy, sugars and oils, and fewer grains and beans. This observation raises two problems that we could be faced with in a future with more people and with higher incomes worldwide.

The first problem concerns our environment, and the second our health.

Many thinkers in the past 200 years have been worried that we might not be able to produce enough food on our Earth to feed a growing population. And there's another worry: whether we can produce our food in a way that does not harm our environment.

One of the greatest threats to our survival on Planet Earth could be climate change. And food has no small role to play here. Currently almost a third of all climate-change-causing greenhouse gases are emitted during food production. And that proportion is expected to grow in the future, if humans continue to consume meat.

Beef is by far the greatest culprit. Cows produce greenhouse gases in their digestion system by fermenting feed in their rumen, the first compartment of their stomachs. Yes, I'm talking about burping and farting! In addition, growing feed for cows and other livestock requires fertilizers, which also emit greenhouse gases. As a result, beef produces about 250 times more greenhouse gases per gram of protein than crops such as lentils and beans, and more than 20 times more greenhouse gases per serving than vegetables. Other animal-based foods – such as eggs, dairy, pork, poultry and some seafood – emit significantly less greenhouse gas than beef, while plant-based foods emit the least.

It is no surprise then that scientists, in order to save our planet, have called for people to move away from diets high in animal products towards more plant-based diets. And the food industry is eager to jump on board with soy-based meat replacements, algae extracts and meats whose production might emit less greenhouse gas – such as lab-grown meat or edible insects. Perhaps you will be one of our future scientists working in this area, helping to produce foods to feed the world without hurting our planet.

Thinking now of health: a move towards plant-based diets could also avoid some of the dangers that come with the otherwise expected increase in meat, dairy, sugars and oils. Processed meats – these include burgers, sausages and chicken nuggets, but also the battered fried fish portion of a plate of fish and chips – have recently been declared carcinogenic. This means that they can cause anyone eating a lot of these foods over a number of years to be more likely to develop cancer in the future. And even unprocessed forms of pork and beef have been associated with greater risks of cancer and other chronic diseases.

At the same time, energy-dense foods that are high in sugars and oils – think of ultra-processed foods such as biscuits, crisps, chips, sugary drinks and the like – are contributing to more people becoming overweight and obese, which is also associated with a greater risk of cancer and other chronic diseases. Sometimes those foods are described as 'empty calories' – calories without any nutritional value. They do not make us feel full, and we often snack on them between meals. Others call such foods 'junk foods'. I bet you can guess why.

Where does all this leave us? It seems clear that to avoid dangerous levels of climate change and unhealthy levels of diet-related diseases, the food of the future needs to deviate from the past trends of eating more and more meat, dairy, sugars and oils. A healthy and environmentally friendly diet for the future would be low in unhealthy and emissions-intensive foods – such as most animal products and ultra-processed foods that are high in sugars and oils – but high in health-promoting and low-intensity foods, such as whole grains, nuts, fruits, vegetables and legumes.

On your next trip to Mars, how about, instead of a beef burger with fries, you try a lentil-and-bean burger in a wholewheat bun with some extra slices of lettuce and tomato? Throw in a toothpaste-like tube of algae if you feel fancy. And enjoy your favourite fruit as dessert. *Bon appétit!*

The Future of Politics Is ... you!

ANDY TAYLOR

Political and Legislative Consultant,
Fellow of the Royal Society of Arts

Politics is about power. It's true that a few people want power because they are bossy and like the sound of their own voices, or they think other people will be impressed by them. But you find such people in other places too. The important thing is that most people who work in politics want to use their power to do good things, to help people and to make their neighbourhood, their country and the world a better place. Using the power of a whole country to put your ideas into practice is one of the best ways of making big changes happen – like tackling climate change or introducing exciting new technology. However, to be successful, you can't just be right; you also need to convince other people to agree with you.

Listening to Politicians

With the power given to them by voters, politicians can do things that other people and organizations can't. They can pass laws that everybody has to abide by, and they can make everybody pay taxes, and spend that money on their ideas. That means considering many different views and judging which ideas are likely to work – which is why debating is such an important part of politics. Robust arguments are a sign of a healthy democracy – as long as people are debating what is best for the country, not just calling each other rude names!

People worry that politicians don't say what they mean. Politicians find it very hard to admit to making mistakes or saying that there are things they don't know, even though they are human like the rest of us. To them, admitting they are not perfect feels very difficult because they have so many political opponents and journalists watching their every move, waiting for them to slip up.

To avoid this problem, some politicians may fall into the trap of saying everything is perfect; they may also avoid answering simple questions or taking responsibility for their decisions. Some try to divert attention from their own mistakes by shouting loudly about their opponents, and some try to disguise their own opinions as facts that can't be challenged. Listening to the arguments can teach you a lot, and the politicians who are the most open and honest about their opinions, and who want to do the right thing, usually end up looking better than those trying to dodge questions.

Trying Out Your Own Opinions

A good start is to try reading or listening to a politician's views on an issue you are interested in – maybe something mentioned in this book, or something else: perhaps protecting endangered tigers or stopping pollution on beaches. You could follow news stories on TV or via downloads, read a number of different newspapers or follow the debates on social media.

Think about which parts you agree with and which you don't. Find other people who are talking about the same issue, and see what you think. Do you agree, or do you have a different opinion? It can be just as much fun finding people you really disagree with. Try to spot when you think a politician is not giving a straight answer, or is making their answer deliberately complicated, or when they claim something as an absolute fact when it is actually just their opinion.

In maths, there's only one right answer to a sum. In physics, you know that if you throw an apple into the air it will definitely fall back to the Earth. Politics, however, is about making your own judgements, working out what you think and then making the case for others to agree with you. Remember too that you can also change your mind as you learn more about an issue.

How You Can Change the World

Having opinions is good, but it doesn't change anything by itself. If you want something important to change, you have to find who has the power to make the right decisions. You might want to ban plastic bags – well, who is responsible for making new laws? Or you might want a new sports ground in your neighbourhood – who is responsible for paying for that?

Remember that politicians don't have to listen to just you – they have lots of different people coming to them with problems and ideas. They only have a limited amount of time and money, and it can be tricky to make the right decision.

Make Your Voice Heard!

Just as politicians need support to get elected, you need to show that your idea works and will be popular. You might join an organization that is already working on the issues you are passionate about. You might want to start a petition – a list signed by all the people who agree with your idea, and presented to a politician or other leader who could do something about the subject of your petition. You could write to your local newspaper. The most important thing is to find people and organizations who believe in the same things you believe in and have the same goal to get something done.

In the past, politics has been controlled by small groups of people who decided what they thought was best for everyone. Looking ahead, I believe that the brightest future for politics and for the strength of our democracies is for us to embrace an idea called pluralism. This means involving many different people in making political decisions, listening to various points of view, and encouraging everybody to take an active interest in the decisions made about the place – town, country, planet – where they live.

The first step in achieving pluralism is for as many people as possible to get involved. That includes you. You might first become an active follower of politics, working out what you believe and what you think needs to change. When you're old enough, you'll have the important responsibility of voting at elections. You might even become a supporter or campaigner for the issues you are passionate about – and perhaps one day you'll be elected as a politician and make the big decisions yourself.

However you get involved, you have the same right to an opinion as everybody else, and an equal right for your voice to be heard.

Cities of the Future

BETH WEST

Head of Development for London, Landsec Real Estate

When you ask people to imagine what the city of the future will look like, most have an idea of what they expect. My idea started with a cartoon that was first shown in 1962 called *The Jetsons*. Living in 2062, the Jetson family had a flat in a very tall apartment building, everyone rode around in flying cars, Mr Jetson worked for only 2 hours per week, and the dog was walked on a treadmill rather than outside. Several concepts shown in *The Jetsons* have already come true: they talked to each other through their televisions (videoconferencing/Skype/FaceTime) and read their newspapers on their television screens as well (iPads/Kindles).

Whatever you think future cities will be like when we reach 2062 or 2081 or beyond, they will keep evolving and there are many challenges that will need to be addressed in order to make cities liveable places in the future.

The modern city – places in which a large proportion of the world's population now make their homes – has been around for less than 200 years. Although cities have existed for over 5,000 years, only 2% of the global population lived in them as recently as 1800. As the Industrial Revolution changed how we made and grew things, more and more people moved into our cities. Two hundred years later, at the beginning of the twenty-first century, over 50% of the global population was living in cities. In the most developed countries in the world, about 75% of people live in cities. By 2030, it is estimated that 67% of the global population and about 85% of people in the most developed countries will be living in cities!

So, if the vast majority of us are going to be living in the cities of the future, what do we need to do to make them truly liveable places for the benefit of all of their residents?

As with many areas of the future, technology will have a big role to play, and many of the different elements of life will need to work together to create somewhere that we want to call home.

In the past, adding more and more people to our cities has resulted in extensive pollution, traffic jams, housing shortages and huge demands on services. City planners of the future will need to consider how to manage these issues if they want to make cities great places, rather than places that we only tolerate because that's where our jobs are.

Where will we live, work and go to school in these cities of the future? What will those experiences be like? Will we have robot butlers? Will we have to work at all, or will everything be done by robots?

As we have seen since the beginning of the Industrial Revolution, many jobs that previously were undertaken by people have been mechanized. There is no reason to think that this trend will change in the future. But there will continue to be a need for people to design the machines and the robots that we will use to do many of these tasks. And lots of things can't be done by machines: creative jobs such as writing books and creating art; designing buildings or computer games. These areas will continue to need people and their ideas. Maybe we'll work fewer days per week in the future, but people could then spend more time with their families, helping their communities or having fun.

No matter what jobs we may be doing, we'll still need a place to do this work. Although technology continues to develop so that a lot of our work can be done from anywhere with an internet connection, many people still choose to go to offices or other spaces where they can collaborate with others. So we're likely to continue to want some kind of building in which to talk to each other and share ideas. As more and more high-rise office buildings are being developed around the world, it is unlikely that our skylines will change completely in future, but these offices are likely to be designed to be attractive places to work. There is increasing demand for outdoor spaces in office towers, so although the skyline may not change, it is likely to look much greener than it currently does, with terraces, roof gardens and green walls.

Different cities have already shown different approaches to where we live – some cities have lots of houses, while others have lots of apartment buildings. As cities become more densely populated, it is likely that housing will need to be intensified, meaning that more people will need to live in the same small area. City planners will need to consider how to develop additional housing – and make it affordable for all types of people to live there – to meet the needs of growing populations.

Whatever the outsides of our houses look like, however, technological changes are likely to make the insides different from today. Many of the devices that currently exist will continue to develop to make our lives easier: smart devices should be able to tell us how much energy we use so that we can use less; other technology can turn on our music or let the cat out. And 2017's Alexa will likely develop into a full-scale robot butler to take care of many more of our household chores.

Schools will also take advantage of changes in technology. Will we need to go into a school building? For the same reason that people prefer to go to offices, children of the future will probably still attend school and teachers will still be humans rather than robots. But technology will develop in ways that allow for virtual and augmented reality that allows children to 'go' to the rainforest or experience the French Revolution or the Roman Empire more than we can today.

So if we know what we're doing in the future with regard to work and school and home, what else needs to be considered so that our cities can be amazing places to live? The big issues affecting cities today are likely to continue to be the big issues of the future: transport and our environment. If our cities are getting bigger and more populated, it will be harder for people to move around easily in cars. Public transport will be key to minimizing the number of people stuck in traffic. Planners will need to consider if more underground trains make sense, or if alternative transport solutions are preferable. Driverless vehicles are likely to be more and more prominent, but will these cars create more traffic or less? We will need to come up with solutions to manage driverless vehicles more effectively, rather than this simply resulting in more cars on the road.

Missed the discussion about driverless cars? Turn to page 368.

Will we need to care about traffic and public transport at all if there are flying cars? Probably even more so. Just because cars can fly, it doesn't mean that traffic and pollution will go away. Combine flying cars with delivery drones and aeroplanes and helicopters, and there could be some very busy and polluted skies!

Transport uses a lot of energy, which has an impact on the environment. Putting millions of people in a single city location is going to have an impact on the environment as they cook, turn on lights, heat and/or cool their homes, charge their phones, use computers and TVs, and travel around. All these things require energy, and energy consumption has historically had a negative effect on the environment.

Many city governments are now looking at how they can lessen their impact on the environment, especially by reducing pollution that could be harming their residents. Effort will need to go into reducing energy consumption and finding environmentally friendly energy solutions to deliver our needs. More and more electricity is generated through renewable and low-carbon means, but really innovative solutions may be the best ways to create the energy we need for the future: hydrogen cars could replace existing petrol and diesel cars (though production of hydrogen comes with its own issues), and their only exhaust would be water vapour rather than carbon dioxide. Technology could be developed that turns human power, generated by walking or cycling, into electricity. Or that turns our homes, offices and schools into energy generators in some way, allowing us each to self-generate our own requirements. Perhaps you, in the future, will be one of those who will design technology like this, or will help in planning and building our cities of the future. A strong vision of what we want these cities to be like will be required so that we can capture all the benefits that technology could give us in our lives. Do you have this vision? I began by imagining my city of the future based on a TV cartoon series. What sort of city can you imagine?

Maybe not flying cars, but hopefully lots of robot butlers!

The Internet: Privacy, Identity and Information

DAVE KING

Chief Executive Officer, Digitalis

ave you ever thought about who can see what you do on the internet or how long the messages you write will last for?

The internet is made up of many, many different computers all interconnected across the world. We tend to access the internet through our mobile phones and other devices but some computers are designed specifically to store the information we all put on the internet. These computers, called servers, host the websites we access. Some of them are in homes and offices, but most are in purpose-built centres run by internet service providers (for short, ISPs). Big companies like Google, Facebook and Amazon have their own data centres – and networks of machines which each hold huge amounts of data. Social media sites allow people to talk to each other using this vast computer network, often over great distances – and much of the content posted to social media platforms is kept, potentially forever! Other messaging applications are deliberately designed to allow for information to be around for only a short while, but of course if you receive a message from somebody electronically you can always find a way to copy it – so things can always find their way on to the internet.

Search engines such as Google use software scripts called robots or 'spiders' to trawl every page of the internet (or certainly as many as they can find) by bouncing continuously from links on one page to another. Their aim is to catalogue everything that is on the web so that we can easily and quickly find what we're looking for.

Search engines and other such sites are therefore constantly copying and listing much of the content we post or read online. In this way something we publish in one place might quickly appear or be recorded somewhere else. As a result, an item published on one site and then removed might already exist on another website – to be found by another internet user at some point in the future.

This is why we should all think really carefully about what to put on the internet about ourselves, because sometimes there is effectively no 'delete' button.

Watch Out!
Information Alert

Telling your friends on social media that you're away on a fantastic holiday with your parents may seem like a really cool thing to do, but the last thing anyone wants is to alert criminals to the fact that their house is empty.

There are other reasons why we might not want people finding information we posted online a long time ago. In the past, as part of job interviews, potential employers would ask previous employers for information about candidates. Nowadays, when you apply for a job, it is common for employers to look you up on social media to find out what they can about you, your friends and what you spend your time doing. This means that what your friends post online – what appears on your timeline, for example – can also have a real impact on what others think about you!

The internet as a whole, and social media especially, has revolutionized our ability to communicate, to have fun and to engage with others. Some people say social media makes us more antisocial in the real world and some use it so much that maybe it does. Like most things, though, if it doesn't take over our lives and we understand the risks of using it, there are many benefits to be had. There are no hard and fast rules, of course, but I created the rules below as a set of things to think about when it comes to sharing your life online.

Seven
Golden Rules

1. Think Before You Post

Before you post something online, don't just think of the person who you intend to see it. Think about whether you're happy for other people – those who know you, and many who don't – to see its content, now or in the future. If in any doubt, don't post!

2. Think Before You Click

There are lots of reasons why people send 'spam' emails to huge lists of people who didn't want or request them. Sometimes they're simply designed to sell products, but other times they contain links designed to take you to a website you shouldn't be visiting. The worst type of spam email attempts to install software on your machine in order to steal data or take control of it. There's a simple rule here. If you're not absolutely sure who an email is from, or if it looks in any way fishy, don't click on any links.

3. Think Before You Share

Many people post pictures to social media without thinking about it, but often the people in those photographs may not be so excited about them being publicly available. Before posting a snap of your brother, sister, parents or friends, why not ask for their permission? After all, it's data about them you're putting out for the world to see. Ask for the same respect from those who take photos – or videos – of you, and never be shy about asking someone not to post. For instance, if you have a party at your house, you might ask all your friends to agree in advance not to post any photos. It could be you who appears on the internet just as you drop a slice of messy pizza all down your chin!

4. Only Befriend Friends

People can pretend to be somebody else over the internet – sometimes by using false names, photographs and ages. These people often rely on the fact that we all want to be popular – and many people will click 'accept' just to add another friend to their count. If you've set up your privacy settings properly, friends can probably see a lot more than those who aren't linked to you, so if you don't know who the person is, don't let them into your circle of trust.

5. Be Aware of Privacy Settings

Social media sites make money by selling advertisement space to companies and brands who want to sell their products. They can make these adverts really powerful and effective by presenting them to people they know are interested in a particular subject. Because of how much we tell them about ourselves they can promise their advertisers that the football-computer-game advert will only be shown to people who talk about football and about games consoles. The downside (for us) is that it's in the interests of these companies for us to put lots of information about ourselves online. All these sites have privacy settings, but they tend to change quite frequently, and most people don't read the details before accepting. The best bet is either to stay on top of this or to assume that anything you post might later be visible to others.

6. Be Aware of Location Settings

Watch out too for location settings, which are certainly helpful when we look on a search engine for a local cinema or skate park. They're less ideal if, when we post thoughts or photos to social media, we don't want other people to know where we are. Did you know that the settings on many apps now default to sharing your location with the app provider? You should always work out whether this will actually make the app more useful to you (if you are using it for directions, for instance, the answer would be yes), whether you trust those who provide the app you are using, and whether that data could fall into the wrong hands. If in doubt, switch it off.

7. Passwords and Security

Software scripts are used by criminals to try many thousands of word combinations in an attempt to 'guess' passwords and get access to people's data. This is why it's so important to use complex passwords (which use more than simple word forms). Thankfully, in years to come, biometric data (like your fingerprint or eyeball scan) will increasingly replace passwords, but for now it's important to come up with a series of passwords which are impossible to guess and complicated for a computer to work out. Never use 'password', '123456' or similarly easy-to-guess patterns. And it's a good idea to avoid something obvious like the name of your pet or your favourite football team, since this information is easy to find out.

Finally, I like to think of the internet as being just like the real world. There are loads of great things going on out there, and so many friendly people. In certain places in the real world, though, we have to learn to be careful where we walk, whom we speak to and what we do. All this works when we're taking a stroll online too.

Climate Change

NITYA KAPADIA

illions of years ago, before humans existed on Earth, there were plants and animals everywhere. These organisms went through the cycle of life and death, and when they died they fell to the ground. As more species fell and rotted away, they were covered by sediment and mud, tiny fragments of eroded minerals carried by wind and water. As the covering layers grew, the temperature increased so it was much hotter and there was a lot more pressure. The rising temperature and pressure eventually transformed these dead organisms into fossil fuels. They remained in the ground for an incredibly long time – millions of years.

Did you know that we have a leap year every 4 years? In a million years there are 997,268 leap years!

Fossil Fuels

There are three fossil fuels: oil, coal and natural gas. In our society today, they have an enormous value because they are our primary sources of energy. We use them to light our homes in the dark, drive our cars and heat us during cold winters. However, to obtain this energy, we have to burn these fossil fuels and, when we do so, they release carbon dioxide, which is a greenhouse gas. This causes problems for our environment because these gases trap heat from the Sun in our Earth's atmosphere, which leads to the temperature rising. This is known as climate change.

Greenhouse Gases

You will probably know that a greenhouse is a building made of glass, which allows plants inside it to keep warm. Heat from the Sun passes through the glass, but the glass keeps out cold winds, ice and snow. This means gardeners can enjoy growing delicate or tropical plants that would be killed in a cold climate. Some gases, such as carbon dioxide, methane and nitrous oxide, work in the same way when they get into Earth's atmosphere. They absorb and emit infrared radiation, trapping heat, so scientists call them 'greenhouse gases'.

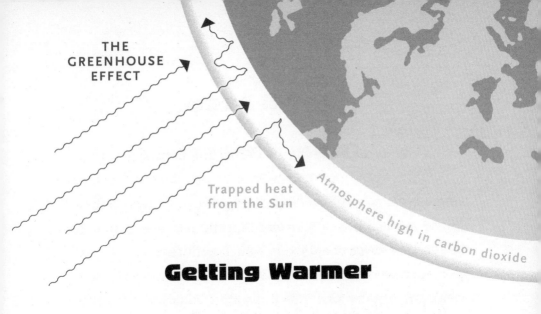

Trapped heat
from the Sun

Atmosphere high in carbon dioxide

Getting Warmer

Now while having hotter weather during a harsh winter might sound appealing, it has started to have a disastrous impact on our planet. As the Earth warms, glaciers and ice caps, which are large bodies of ice, are melting. Not only does this lead to a significant loss of habitat for several species that live on the ice, so many animals lose their homes, it also means that many peoples, living in coastal areas and on low-lying islands, will find the sea level rising. Their homes and their lands will be liable to severe flooding. Some may be lost completely.

In addition to these problems, the melting of the ice caps has another effect on climate change. The colour white, which is the colour of the ice caps and glaciers, reflects heat out of our atmosphere. As more ice melts, there is less ice reflecting less heat out of our atmosphere. The heat remains trapped on the Earth's surface and so the Earth's temperature climbs further up. Some scientists believe that there is a 'tipping point' beyond which our planet can still be habitable. I find this deeply shocking, because this means that our way of living might come to an end.

Other Threats

Climate change and increased volumes of carbon dioxide in the air also pose other worrying threats. For instance, an increase in carbon dioxide, which pollutes our air, leads to a decrease in air quality. That means that there is less clean and healthy air for us to breathe, which causes many serious health conditions. Furthermore, water quality, which measures how good the water is, will also be reduced because water bodies will be contaminated by pollutants like carbon dioxide. This does not just affect humans – all life on Earth is impacted by these problems. The diversity of species on our planet is in dramatic decline, with experts estimating that we are losing between 0.01% to 0.1% of our species every year. These numbers do not really seem that high but when you put into context that there are millions of species on our planet, it is an enormous number.

Did you know that scientists calculate that clams in the Baltic Sea release as much of the greenhouse gas methane as 20,000 cows?

A Weather Forecast

Moreover, as the Earth warms up, weather patterns will be hugely affected. At the same time as more precipitation (rain, snow, sleet or hail) falls in some areas of the world, other places are starting to experience very serious droughts. Because of these much harsher heat waves and droughts, many regions will be left with lower volumes of water available, insufficient for everyday use. Some areas will become completely uninhabitable. This change in weather patterns will have a very marked impact on human life and water shortages could even be the cause of wars breaking out in the future. The world will also have to combat more frequent natural disasters such as hurricanes and floods.

What can we do?

We hear a great deal about single-use plastics, but fossil fuels are also single-use – they are non-renewable sources of energy, which means we can only use them once. As we look to the future, we need to start using renewable energy, such as solar or wind energy. These are much more eco-friendly as they do not emit greenhouse gases. The solutions to problems related to climate change are admittedly quite complex but that doesn't mean we shouldn't try.

Trees and Plants

Plants take nutrients from sunlight, air and water by a process called 'photosynthesis'. In doing this, they capture large amounts of carbon dioxide. In fact, at the moment the only sure way of getting carbon dioxide out of the atmosphere is through photosynthesis!

Trees take up more carbon dioxide than any other single plant. If we could plant many more trees than we have, it would be enormously useful in helping to lessen the effect of greenhouse gases. All trees are good, but trees that grow quickly and live a long time, such as horse chestnuts, walnuts and various pines, are extra good.

Peat, a type of soil made from wet and partly rotten plant material, is also very good at retaining carbon dioxide.

However, if a tree is cut down or burned, it will release all its stored carbon dioxide back into the atmosphere! If peat is cut and dried, to use as fuel or as compost for gardens, it will also release carbon dioxide.

If you haven't got a garden to plant a tree in, why not grow a potted plant or two? Even a small plant will help, if you look after it properly.

Nothing should deter you from wanting to help and taking action, regardless of your age or location. For inspiration, look at Greta Thunberg, a climate change activist who was nominated for the Nobel Peace Prize at aged 16. The reason so many people in our generation find her very inspirational is because she is so young. Rather than her age becoming a barrier for preventing the climate crisis, she uses it as an opportunity to highlight the severity of our problems.

In order to do something, it is crucial that you educate yourself on the various different causes and consequences of climate change. While fossil fuels are one of the main issues, there are several challenges that we need to consider, such as plastic polluting the ocean and killing organisms. What we do now with our planet, when we are at such a tipping point, will affect all future generations. It is imperative that we take action now.

I find our environmental issues terrifying! It is as if there is a clock, counting down on life in our world. So many of our problems seem so complicated, and so far out of our capacity to make change. I know that, like me, many people in my age group feel a sense of helplessness considering it will take a huge effort to tackle our problems, which go far beyond just one individual's ability to solve. Personally, I do not believe it should just concern the younger generations, but instead should involve all generations. These problems threaten our way of life, and if no action is taken, in a few years we could be living completely different lives. It is frightening to think that unless we take immediate action, such as changing our energy sources from fossil fuels to cleaner, renewable sources, we will have to face consequences such as less food being produced to feed the world, or water wars.

However, I believe that we can solve our problems by coming together and creating practical and effective solutions. If I had to make one major change in the world today to prevent climate change, I would want to stop deforestation. This includes enforcing rules to ensure that paper and other resources from the forest are obtained sustainably, and that when trees are cut down new ones are planted at once to replace them. Reforesting is very important because not only are these forests home to so many species, forests emit oxygen for us to breathe. If you could make any change, what would you do?

Afterword

I've never liked saying goodbyes. It always seems too sad and too final. But there are a couple of important farewells to say with this book. My beloved father, Stephen, is no longer with us and is so very badly missed – by me and by millions of others. And my great friend, collaborator, supporter and all-round science genius Peter McOwan recently passed away. The light feels a bit dimmer and greyer without these two, both great scientists and wonderful human beings who sought to use their own intelligence and insight to create a better, fairer world. Both would have been so delighted to read the work of our authors, including our youngest ever contributor, Nitya, a teenage climate change activist who has written for us on how the future looks to her generation. So, while my heart breaks that these two amazing people are not with us, I console myself with the thought that we have their work and their lives as sources of inspiration and knowledge – and that there is a new generation of passionate, engaged and outspoken young scientists and activists emerging. My father and Peter would have been so proud of them. They might just save the world. And so could you.

Lucy Hawking

Glossary

algorithm A set of rules to be followed when working out a problem. Computers use algorithms when they are calculating.

altitude The distance of an object in the sky above (or sometimes below) the horizon, measured as an angle. The height of a satellite above the Earth, measured in kilometres or miles, is also described as its altitude.

analogue computer An analogue computer uses data from physical sources that are continuous but changing, such as temper-atures, mechanical movements or voltages. Most analogue computers have now been replaced by digital computers.

analogy A comparison between two things, usually to explain something or make it clearer.

android A robot that is made to look like a human being.

antimatter Ordinary matter is made up of particles – electrons, protons and neutrons. Antimatter is the opposite: it is made up of positrons, antiprotons and anti-neutrons. The particles of matter and antimatter have equal but opposite electrical charges, and if they were to meet, they would destroy each other, leaving only energy.

ASCII The American Standard Code for Information Interchange. First used in telecommunications, it is a code used in computing, though modern coding has developed considerably from the original version.

binary system, binary solar system A binary system describes two stars that orbit each other. Gravity attracts the two stars, and their paths are ellipses, not circles. Sirius, the Dog Star, the brightest star in the sky, is a binary system.

bioengineering Genetic engineering, when certain charac-teristics are deliberately introduced into a living organism. For example, scientists might add genes that enable a grain like wheat or rice to withstand drought or cold, so more can be grown in places that would otherwise be hard to farm. Bioengineering can also be used to describe giving people artificial organs that make them work better – these might include hearing aids or artificial limbs.

biominerals Living things can produce minerals, often used to harden their existing tissues. These minerals are known as biominerals, and include shells and skeletons.

black smoker A hole (or vent) on the seabed from which superheated water is ejected. The water is black because it contains sulphides, black compounds of sulphur.

blue shift When a source of light moves, it creates waves. The waves of visible light can come in different lengths. When a light source is moving fast towards an observer, the wavelengths are short, and look blue. This is known as a blue shift. (When the light source travels away from an observer, the wavelengths get longer and look red – a red shift.) Using the colour of the wavelengths, it's possible to tell in which direction a light source is travelling.

cosmos, cosmocentric
Cosmos is another word for the Universe, and sometimes it is used to refer to space. Words that start 'cosmo' have to do with the Universe. Cosmocentric describes the idea that the Universe is the most important thing, the opposite of 'anthropocentric', which thinks that human existence is the most important thing. A cosmocentric view of nature would object to actions like people redesigning planets so they could live on them.

cryogenic To do with very low temperatures – being at a low temperature, or producing a low temperature, or related to a low temperature. Cryogenics is a branch of physics that studies the subject.

cryovolcano When a cryovolcano erupts, it pours out things such as water, methane or ammonia rather than molten rock. The eruptions can be in liquid or vapour form, but freeze solid when they condense. Scientists think there are cryo-volcanoes on Pluto and some of the moons far out in the Solar System, such as Saturn's moons Titan and Enceladus.

cryptography Secret writing. It usually refers to putting messages into code, or decoding messages that are sent in ciphers.

cybersecurity Keeping safe data that is stored electronically on computers. Organizations of all kinds want to protect information from anyone who has no right to have it or use it, including criminals.

diaphragm A partition. In mammals, it refers to muscles that separate the neck from the chest area. It can also describe such things as a device for varying the lens aperture in a camera, or a thin membrane making a partition in a sound system.

EDSAC The Electronic Delay Storage Automatic Calculator. An early British computer. It was built at Cambridge University, and was taken up by J. Lyons & Co., a company involved in the catering business. Lyons was the first British company to use a computer commercially.

electromagnetic radiation A form of energy found throughout the Universe. It moves in the form of waves. These range from radio waves, which have the longest wavelengths, through microwaves, infrared, visible light, ultraviolet, X-rays and gamma rays, which have the shortest wavelength.

empathy The ability to understand and be sensitive to the thoughts and feelings of another being, without having them explained.

epiphany A moment of sudden understanding or revelation.

ESA The European Space Agency. ESA is a group of 22 countries dedicated to exploring space. ESA's headquarters are in Paris. ESA is involved in manned and unmanned space flight, including the International Space Station and the Orion spacecraft destined for future Moon landings.

fundamental particles The smallest things in the Universe. They make up the electrons, protons and neutrons that form atoms.

fuse To join different things together so they become one. This is often done by using heat, which melts the different elements so they mix.

geocentric Having the Earth at the centre. Early astronomers and scholars thought everything in the heavens – the Sun, the Moon and the stars – revolved round the Earth, which they believed was in the middle of everything.

greenhouse gas A gas like carbon dioxide, which builds up in Earth's atmosphere and stops heat escaping. This causes the atmosphere to become hotter. Methane is another greenhouse gas.

hydrothermal vent A hole in the seabed from which flows very hot water full of minerals. A black smoker is a type of hydrothermal vent.

hyperspace A space of more than three dimensions. In stories, it is an imaginary place where it would be possible to travel faster than light.

ion Usually an atom that has lost at least one of its electrons. This gives it a positive electrical charge. An atom with an extra electron is an ion with a negative electrical charge. Atoms can become ions when they collide with each other.

Kuiper belt An area of the Solar System stretching far out into space from the orbit of Neptune. It is full of small icy objects – frozen water, methane and ammonia – that are probably left over from the formation of the Solar System.

latitude An imaginary line round the Earth, parallel to the Equator. It is used to measure distances from the Equator in degrees. There are 90 degrees of latitude on each side of the Equator.

logarithm Numbers that can be used to express repeated multiplications of a single number. For example, 2 x 2 x 2 can be written as 2^3. A mathematician would call 2 the base number, and 3 the exponent. 3 is the logarithm of the number 8 to the base 2.

longitude An imaginary line round the Earth. Lines of longitude run north and south, starting at the North Pole and running to the South Pole. They are measured in degrees, beginning at the Greenwich meridian in London, which is 0 degrees longitude.

macroscopic Something described as macroscopic can be seen with ordinary eyesight. It doesn't need to be magnified to be visible. Sometimes 'macroscopic' is used for an object on a very large scale.

nanotechnology 'Nano' means something so tiny it is sub-microscopic. Nanotechnology describes technology at an atomic or molecular scale, and a nanobot is a very small self-propelled machine. The nanoworld is the area of science where minute things are studied or made.

NASA The National Aeronautics and Space Administration. An American government agency, NASA is responsible for all American space flights, space probes and satellites. It also carries out research and runs launch sites.

neurone Cell that transmits the impulses of the nerves. Almost every species of animal has neurones.

node In astronomy, a node is a crossing point. It is the point where the orbit of a heavenly body, such as a planet or a moon, crosses a plane being used for reference, such as the plane of Earth's orbit, or the celestial equator.

particle One of the very tiny pieces of matter that make up an atom. Varying numbers of protons, neutrons and electrons make up different kinds of atoms.

phyllocian period Part of the chronology (or timeline) of the history of Mars. Scientists try to work out when different events occurred, which are the oldest rocks and land formations, and what might have happened more recently. Using information gathered by the Mars Express probe, scientists have looked at the way surface minerals have been changed by weathering. The Phyllocian period covers a time when there was water on the surface of Mars, valleys were formed and deposits of clay were left on the surface. Scientists think that if there is any evidence of life on Mars, it will come from this time in its history. Phylloscilicate is the name of a type of clay.

plasma A cloud of gas full of ions – a mixture of electrons and the nuclei of atoms. Everything inside stars is in a state of plasma.

psychology The study of the human mind and how it works, with particular reference to the way people behave.

radioactive A kind of energy. This energy is given out when a radioactive atom throws out one or more particles, such as protons

or neutrons. When the Universe
was created enormous amounts of
radioactivity were released.

space–time A mathematical
framework which uses four dimensions to locate any event or object.
It is based on the speed of light,
which never changes and therefore
can be used to measure time, plus
three-dimensional space, joined
together.

supernova When a very large old
star runs out of nuclear fuel, the
material that is left collapses
inwards. The temperature at the
centre of the star increases by
millions of degrees, and it explodes
in a supernova. The light from a
supernova can be up to 20 times
brighter than the light from the
original star.

velocity the speed with which an
object moves in one direction.
Velocity is measured by length
and time, for example metres per
second, or miles per hour.

wave function How waves behave.
A wave is a form of energy, which
oscillates – it moves up and down,
or backwards and forwards, in a
steady pattern. Electromagnetic
radiation travels in waves.

INDEX

ACKNOWLEDGEMENTS

Special thanks to Dr Toby Blench, Sue Cook, Dr Christophe Galfard, Stuart Rankin and Felicity Trotman for their invaluable editorial assistance and input in different editions of the George series and on *Unlocking the Universe*.

A huge and warm thank you to everyone at Penguin Random House Children's for believing in the George series and working so hard to publish books that make science accessible to young readers! In particular, Ruth Knowles, Emma Jones and Annie Eaton. Also a massive thank you for all the brilliant backup from the team at Janklow and Nesbit, led by Rebecca Carter.

'What You Need to Know about Black Holes' by Professor Stephen Hawking was first published in *George's Secret Key to the Universe* (Corgi Books, 2007)

'Why Do We Go into Space?' by Professor Stephen Hawking, 'A Voyage Across the Universe' by Professor Bernard Carr, 'Getting in Touch with Aliens' by Dr Seth Shostak, 'Did Life Come from Mars?' by Dr Brandon Carter, 'Is There Anyone Out There?' by Lord Martin Rees were first published in *George's Cosmic Treasure Hunt* (Corgi Books, 2009)

'The Creation of the Universe' by Professor Stephen Hawking, 'The Dark Side of the Universe' by Dr Paul Davies, 'Wormholes and Time Travel' by Dr Kip S. Thorne were first published in *George and the Big Bang* (Corgi Books, 2011)

'My Robot, Your Robots' by Professor Peter McOwan, 'The History of Life' by Professor Michael J. Reiss, 'Quantum Computers' by Dr Raymond Laflamme, 'The Building Blocks of Life' by Dr Toby Blench, '3D Printing' by Dr Tim Prestidge were first published in *George and the Unbreakable Code* (Corgi Books, 2014)

'The Oceans of Earth' by Professor Ros E. M. Rickaby, 'Volcanoes on Earth, in our Solar System and Beyond' by Professor Tamsin A. Mather, 'Building Rockets for Mars' by Allyson Thomas, 'Imagining a Life on Mars' by Kellie Gerardi, 'The Overview Effect' by Dr Richard Garriott de Cayeux were first published in *George and the Blue Moon* (Corgi Books, 2016) 'Buildings Rockets for Mars' copyright © 2015 National Aeronautics and Space Administration, an Agency of the United States Government. Used with Permission.

'Time Travel and the Mystery of the Moving Clocks' by Professor Peter McOwan, 'The Future of Food' by Dr Marco Springmann, 'The Future of Politics is . . . You!' by Andy Taylor, 'Cities of the Future' by Beth West, 'Robot Ethics' by Dr Kate Darling, 'The Internet: Privacy, Identity and Information' by Dave King were first published in *George and the Ship of Time* (Corgi Books, 2018)

First published in this edition: 'Genetics' by Professor Ammar Al Chalabi, 'Flat-Earthers, Moon-Hoaxers and Anti-Vaxxers' by Dr Sophie Hodgetts, 'The Multiverse' by Professor Thomas Hertog, 'Black Holes' by Sasha Haco, 'Artificial Intelligence' by Dr Demis Hassabis, 'On the Ethics of AI' by Carissa Veliz, and 'Climate Change' by Nitya Kapadia

Colour insert credits
Footprint on the Moon, and first photograph of Earth from the Moon © NASA (National Aeronautics and Space Administration, an Agency of the United States Government) All other colour photographs/images © shutterstock

Ready to embark on an INTERGALACTIC adventure?

Discover the incredible series by Lucy and Stephen Hawking

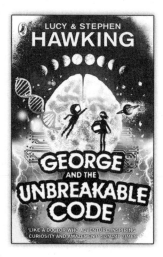